ROUTEMASTER
HANDBOOK

Andrew Morgan

Capital Transport

Introduction

The Routemaster was the last bus to be wholly designed by London Transport for use in the capital. It was designed in the 1950s for the large scale replacement of the London trolleybus fleet. Although it is well known that the Routemaster was more expensive than alternative vehicles available at the time, it proved to be a vehicle with untouchable longevity. Some thought as the last vehicle entered service that the Routemaster design was obsolete, having been effectively killed off by its exclusion from 1960's Bus Grant specification. And who would have thought that hundreds of second-hand Routemasters would have found homes with operators in the 1980s and 1990s?

It is nearly fourteen years since the first large scale withdrawals and sales of Routemasters by London Transport commenced. With the sudden emergence of large numbers of well maintained second-hand vehicles, the Routemaster was to be an obvious choice for would-be owners. But it was with the arrival of Deregulation from 1986 that the Routemaster proved to be a very useful tool in the highly competitive environment, and had the advantage over more modern vehicles of speed of loading and passenger acceptability. Hence large numbers of Routemasters left London for all over Britain. Although most operators have now discontinued their Routemaster operations for one reason or another, the Routemaster continues to have its role to play in bus operation in the mid-1990s.

Nowhere more so than the crowded streets of London, the home of the Routemaster, where there is still the largest number of operational Routemasters. With the completion of the RML refurbishment programme and the privatisation of the London Buses operating companies in 1994, these operations are currently stable until the contracts for the various London Transport Buses routes are renewed between 1997 and 2001 (provisional dates). Additionally environmental enhancements have recently been announced to improve the "greenness" of these vehicles. With all but a few Routemasters now in the hands of private operators, a new chapter has started for the Routemaster in London.

As with other classes of London bus, examples have joined the ranks of preserved vehicles as well as the fleets of miscellaneous vehicles on non-psv duties. Also Routemasters of all varieties, including Airways and Northern General vehicles, have been exported and can be seen in at least 39 countries around the world for just about every conceivable use.

The early Routemasters have now been in psv service for longer than any RT class vehicle, and unless there is a dramatic change of policy, the Routemaster should continue to see service into the next century. This is despite the fact that Routemaster vehicles are between 28 and 38 years old, yet were only built for a 15 year life span. The 8th February 1996 was the 40th anniversary of RM1 entering passenger service on London Transport route 2 (Golders Green to Crystal Palace) and yet another landmark was passed.

This book would not have been possible without the help of people too numerous to mention, but in particular the help given by Maurice Bateman and Keith Hamer. This publication is believed to be as accurate and up-to-date as possible and readers can keep track of changes by consulting the news sheets of the London Omnibus Traction Society, the PSV Circle or the Routemaster Operators & Owners Association.

Published by Capital Transport Publishing
38 Long Elmes, Harrow Weald, Middlesex

Printed in England

Contents

First published 1992
Second Edition 1996

ISBN 185414 187 2

London Transport's RMF1254 after sale to Northern General. It was photographed in August 1967, nine months after moving to north-east England. The bus gave thirteen years of service to its new owner.
Capital Transport

HISTORY OF DISPOSALS

The first sale of a Routemaster by London Transport was of prototype front-entrance RMF1254. It had been built in 1962, but had only been used in London on the BEA service to Heathrow Airport. Additionally it was used as a demonstrator to other potential operators in England. It was ironic that the only order for the Routemaster from outside London came from a company that had not actually tried out this vehicle, namely Northern General of Gateshead. Following on from the order for fifty such vehicles, RMF1254 joined its sisters in November 1966.

Following the successful operation of RMF1254, BEA later purchased a fleet of 65 standard length RMF type vehicles to replace its AEC Regal 1½ deck coaches in 1966/67. British Airways withdrew its fleet of front-entrance Routemasters between 1975 and 1979, London Country its RMCs, RCLs and RMLs by March 1980, and Northern General its RMF type vehicles by 1981, but large scale withdrawals of Routemasters from the capital did not commence until 1982. It was only recently, with the approach of the privatisation of the London Buses subsidiaries and the completion of the RML refurbishment programme that these large scale sales ceased. Instead various vehicles are withdrawn or just pass between operators from the so-called provincial fleets.

Sales of the first standard Routemasters commenced in September 1972 with RML2691, which was sold to Gala Cosmetics for use as a mobile beauty salon with Mary Quant. RMs 50, 304, 1268, 1447 and 1659 were all scrapped in 1974 after fires or collisions. At this time RM1368 also suffered from fire damage and in 1975 the damaged upper deck was removed, and as a single-decker it went to the experimental department at Chiswick works. There it replaced RM8, which had been at Chiswick since it was built in 1958 and now entered service for the first time in 1976. Only two other central area RMLs have been sold, being RMLs 900 and 2557. The latter was fire-damaged in 1983, while the former was an accident victim and was deemed by London Buses to be uneconomical to repair; so in February 1988 the then Clydeside Scottish bought it and rebuilt it at their Johnstone workshops with parts from RM1984. By the end of June 1988 it had re-entered service, but this time north of the Border. This unique RML made a well-publicised visit to London during that month and was used in passenger service on routes 13 and 26 before attending the North Weald Rally. Early in 1995, it was purchased by Blue Triangle at Rainham but at the time of writing it remains in store.

The first quantity disposals from London were dictated by politics. The Labour Party took office on the Greater London Council after the elections of May 1981, and swiftly moved to implement their 'Fares Fair' programme. Fares were cut by an average of 32% on all London Transport buses and the Underground from October 1981 and the passengers daily carried by them rose from $5^1/_2$ to 6 million. The increased subsidy required by London Transport was partly funded from the rates, which in turn had to be increased. This met with opposition from the ratepayers, and the London Borough of Bromley contested the legality of the subsidies in the Courts, with the result that the Law Lords declared them to be unlawful. Consequently, on 21st March 1982, London Transport fares were increased, in effect doubling overnight and thus becoming 33% higher than before the introduction of the Fares Fair policy. Inevitably, passenger journeys dropped back to 5 million per day, which led to the large-scale cuts and service revisions on 4th September, including the initiation of the London Routemaster withdrawals.

The scheduled vehicle requirement was reduced by 220 RMs, 19 RMLs and 5 RCLs by the September revision. By the end of the year 61 RMs had been sold and a further 98 were wholly or partly broken up at Aldenham works. The first of these sales took place in October with 51 being sold for scrap to W. North's of Sherburn-in-Elmet, with parts being returned to London Buses; seven being written off for scrap; and four being exported to Japan. These, RMs 326, 496, 1248 and 1730, had actually left the country in August, initially for display at the Matsuda collection there.

After these unhappy months, withdrawals of Routemasters continued until late 1988, due to the steady conversion of routes to one-person operation. The RML fleet continued to remain intact with RMs being replaced by any surplus RMLs. Despite this massive number of withdrawals, in early 1996, there were just over 700 Routemasters owned by operators in the London area and a peak vehicle requirement (pvr) of 507 on London Transport Buses (LTB) routes alone. Nowadays all routes, except route 13 which is operated by BTS Coaches, operate on Monday to Saturday only. However sales of RMs continued, mostly to scrap dealers, with a few for non-PSV use, and a very few to preservationists and overseas buyers. Unlike the more modern types, which quickly saw further service with operators around the country, no RMs were taken on by any other UK bus company at the start. The first withdrawals were of vehicles fitted with non-standard equipment, e.g. Leyland engines and Simms electrical components. As the overhauls were coming to an end in 1985, the emphasis changed to vehicles that were due for their fifth body overhaul.

In late 1984, RM1288 and 1873 were exported to Hong Kong in the hope that Hong Kong and China might become a large export market. RM1288 was rebuilt at Aldenham works with a nearside staircase and offside platform. Unfortunately the much-rumoured sale of up to 1300 buses to China never materialised and, with another two vehicles exported to Hong Kong in 1991, these remain the only Routemasters to be exported to this part of the Far East.

Until June 1984, the Routemaster had fitted into London Transport's programme at Aldenham works, where the bodies and sub-frames were separated for overhaul. The last vehicle to be treated in this way was RM198. As is well documented elsewhere, the system of overhauls completely mixed all the different batches of vehicles. For example, Leyland-engined vehicles were spread throughout the fleet and low-numbered bodies with non-opening upper-deck front windows could be found on practically any vehicle; but exterior advertisement bodies generally remained on the higher-numbered vehicles. Only the RMAs, RCLs and some RMLs did not have any body changes. So once the system of exchanging bodies on overhaul had ceased, the fleet was 'frozen' in this confused state and remains so to this day.

The following year, Stagecoach, the then independent operator in the Perth area, purchased five Leyland-engined Routemasters which were the first of the type to operate north of the Border. Later that year, Clydeside Scottish Omnibuses Ltd were lent RM652 for an open day and retained it for trials around the Glasgow outskirts. Clydeside was one of the new subsidiaries of the Scottish Bus Group, formed in 1985 in preparation for bus deregulation scheduled for 26th October 1986. After the success of the trials with RM652, Clydeside went on to acquire and operate over 70 Routemasters. Another recently-formed company, Kelvin Scottish, borrowed several Routemasters from Clydeside and then established a fleet of over 50 vehicles. In this way the Scottish Bus Group was able to compete directly with its long time rival Strathclyde PTE. Another new Scottish Bus Group company, Strathtay Scottish, conducted successful trials and acquired over 20 vehicles for use in Perth and Dundee.

Suddenly the Routemaster was seen as the ideal tool in the competitive battle for passengers around the United Kingdom. Their relatively fast operation, combined with a friendly crew, and their reasonable initial costs for a well maintained vehicle were all advantages that made an instant appeal to operators up and down the country.

By deregulation day, most of the initial order for 137 Routemasters for the Scottish Bus Group had been delivered. In Glasgow, both Clydeside and Kelvin introduced new services with them from 31st August; also, from 26th October, Stagecoach set up a new subsidiary in Glasgow named Magicbus, which also started using them. These had been transferred from local contracts, school and other rural services from around their Perth base. Meanwhile, in England, Blackpool Transport purchased six Routemasters in 1986 to augment their existing fleet of crew-operated Leyland PD3s. Later, by buying a further six in 1987, they were able to replace the PD3s altogether.

In the spring of 1986, London Buses itself resurrected fifty vehicles (39 RMs and 11 RCLs) at Aldenham works for use on sightseeing work and repainted them in a 'traditional' livery. These became part of the new Tours and Charter fleet (later renamed London Coaches).

In the summer of 1987, Southampton City Transport acquired a fleet of (initially twelve) Leyland engined vehicles to use against new operator Solent Blue Line. At about the same time, another south coast operator, Verwood Transport, commenced operation using up to three RMAs (11, 37 and 58) in the Bournemouth and Poole areas. Unusually these vehicles were modified and used as one-person operated vehicles. The Verwood Transport services were sold to Wilts & Dorset at the end of January 1989. However, RMA37 was retained by Mr R Brown after the last day of operation on 30th January. It has since been used by Classic Buses on the Hampshire County Council Sunday Rider scheme in the summer of 1989 and more recently with Shaftesbury & District.

With the privatisation of the former National Bus Company subsidiaries, Scottish operator Stagecoach acquired Cumberland Motor Services and United Counties Omnibus Company and commenced Routemaster operation with these companies in Carlisle in October 1987 and in Bedford in February 1988 respectively. Additionally, the United Counties Routemaster operation in Corby commenced in April 1988. A later arrival was former Magicbus RM504 in April 1988, which was the last United Counties vehicle to be painted in the green livery. In May 1988, East Yorkshire started Routemaster operation in Hull, but interestingly not only did they revive crew operation but also the very attractive livery of dark blue, primrose and white. Also, in the same month and in the same town, Citilink commenced operation on local services with RM188 and RM1741. Further new operators continued with Burnley & Pendle commencing operation in March 1988, Southend Transport commencing operation in late August 1988 (having taken various vehicles on loan during 1987) and Greater Manchester Buses in September 1988. Ironically, Manchester Corporation Transport evaluated RM1414 in 1963 only to acquire second hand examples 25 years later.

At the end of 1988, forty Routemasters were exported to the Sri Lanka Transport Board and during 1989/90 some 30 vehicles went to individual owners in Japan. Although these were quite substantial batches, they fell far short of the hundreds of exports that had been talked about earlier.

Other independent operators to acquire Routemasters included Confidence Bus & Coach in Leicester, who had school and university contracts in and around that city. K & M Gagg (Coaches) of Bunny in Nottinghamshire acquired two Routemasters in 1987 and ran services with them around Nottingham. These routes were withdrawn in January 1989 after a deal with Barton Transport, and RM790 was sold in the following September. RM1314 was repainted in the fleet livery of blue, silver and white. It received an unusual refurbishment; the seats were re-trimmed with orange moquette, the burgundy rexine was replaced in a tan colour and it was fitted with interior light bulbs of different colours. As well as being used for school and other contract work, it ran during 1991-1993 on the Sherwood Forester Network. However, it was sold in 1994. Two

Routemasters went to Gash of Newark in October 1986 and another in December 1986. All three operated on local town services 81, 82 and 83. In the summer of 1988, minibuses replaced all the Routemasters, which were transferred to routes 72 and 73. However, with the company now owned by Yorkshire Traction, it was integrated with Lincolnshire Road Car and the Routemasters were sold to East Yorkshire in July 1989. Blue Triangle of Romford (and more recently of Rainham in Essex) acquired several vehicles and have used an RMA, RMC and RCL on tours to rallies as well as Essex contract work, along with their other AEC vehicles. They have also used a former Northern General open-top RMF (FPT588C) for sightseeing work. Pulfrey Tours of Great Gonerby ran RM1109 for six months in 1987 before selling it to Rotherham & District, who occasionally used it in service with RM584. From February 1989 Rotherham & District started working routes in the Sheffield area. In July 1990, they bought eight Routemasters from Greater Manchester Buses – RMs 378, 429, 698, 1604, 1618, 1807, 2162 and 2200. RM378 was sold immediately, while the remaining nine were used to varying degrees. However, their use of Routemasters ended in February 1991 and they were quickly sold. Soon afterwards, the whole Rotherham & District operation ceased altogether. The vehicles were actually owned by Mr G Pegg and were leased to the company.

From 1986 onwards, RMs, notably with Stagecoach and then Kelvin Scottish, have lost their non-suffix registrations with them being sold or transferred to other vehicles. Strathtay even sold two ALDxxxB registrations in 1990 and Kelvin likewise with ALM81B in 1993.

By the end of 1988, further conversions to one-person operation had ended for the time being and London Buses commenced a repaint programme in an attempt to improve the appearance of the remaining fleet.

After years of expansion of Routemaster and crew operation, various companies have rationalised their fleets or have withdrawn them altogether. In preparation for the privatisation of the Scottish Bus Group, Clydeside re-merged with Western in December 1988 and Kelvin merged with Central. The Western management did not see the merits of the Routemaster and for one reason or another announced that the entire fleet would be withdrawn. It was renumbered C10-C84 in January 1989 and the final repaint was carried out in August 1989 on RM166. RML900 and RMA16 (now numbered SRMA1) were retained after the rest of the fleet had been sold, mostly to dealers, by August 1990. In September 1989, RM794 and 835 were hired to Eastern Scottish, who in connection with the Royal Highland Show, hired RMs 110, 835 and 978 from 21st-23rd June 1990. Additionally they hired RM316 (SR25) from Strathtay Scottish for three weeks from 13th August for use on route 99 during the Edinburgh Festival. Withdrawal of the Clydeside Routemasters started in December and RML900 and RM73 were the last vehicles to operate the original services on 27th April. A farewell tour had been held on 11th February but as the new replacements were not fully serviceable, the Routemasters continued for ten more weeks.

Unfortunately it soon became apparent that Kelvin Scottish were suffering from severe financial problems, and from 12th July 1987 the Routemaster fleet was reduced overnight to 40 operational vehicles. The surplus vehicles were then sold off, notably to Stagecoach (for operation in Carlisle) and to Clydeside; and the others were cannibalised for spare parts. After this, there was a period of stability. RM371, had been re-registered to EDS281A in 1988, was re-registered WLT371 again in 1988 when it was repainted as the first all-over advert bus in the fleet. This was the first time that a Routemaster had re-gained its original registration. This has subsequently occurred a further eight times.

In early 1990 several vehicles were withdrawn, and in May of that year six former Clydeside buses were purchased to enable fleet strength to be maintained and to replace those in poor condition. From October 1990, seven RMs were repainted in the new Kelvin Central Buses (KCB) livery of red and ivory which from now on replaced the original two-tone blue and yellow one. The new scheme was very similar to that used by Cumberland Motor Services except that the stripes faced the other way. Following the withdrawal of the western side of the Routemaster operation, sales commenced of the surplus vehicles; notably they were mostly to dealers. However spasmodic operation was common, including from Kirkintilloch depot. A final KCB farewell tour took place on 28th March 1993 with RM367 covering the various routes that the RMs had operated since 1986. However, at least five RMs saw use for another month. Furthermore, RM606 continued in use as a staff bus until June 1994.

A surprise purchase occurred on 10th April 1992 when the Glasgow operations of Stagecoach were acquired by KCB. In addition the two RMAs were included in the deal as well. The former Magicbus operation base at Springburn continued but was converted to one-person operation on 31st July 1993, thereby ending Routemaster operation in Glasgow after some nine years.

RMA16 was repainted in June 1992 and is seen in the following September operating alongside one of the many minibuses competing for passengers in Greenock.
A. Morgan

Moving south, Southampton City Transport withdrew their fleet on 14th January 1989, which was replaced by new vehicles. The alternative to new buses and the ending of crew operation would have been the renovation of the Routemaster fleet, but the company decided against this. Surprisingly, for Christmas 1990, they resurrected RMs 1543 and 1682, which were still in stock, for a 'Shoppa-Hoppa' service between 26th November and 24th December. These vehicles, along with the cannibalised RM2011, were then sold to Southend Transport.

The Greater Manchester Buses operation ceased on 16th June 1990, with RM1136 being the last vehicle. A tour took place on the following day with RMs 429 and 1776. All were then stored although RM1136 and 1776 saw very occasional use the following month. The Burnley & Pendle 'Eastenders' operation ceased on 21st December 1990 and all the vehicles were stored until the summer of 1992.

Only one of Gash's three Routemasters received the company's own livery. It is seen in June 1989 after the company had been taken over by Road Car. *A. Morgan*

During the summer of 1992, two Routemasters featured as part of the Nottinghamshire County Council Sherwood Forester network. Unfortunately Gagg's RM1314 and East Midland's RM1164 do not make good examples of how to use the ample blind displays built into the Park Royal Routemaster bodywork. Both vehicles have subsequently been sold. *P. D Scott*

The operation of Routemasters with Greater Manchester Buses lasted nearly three years. Like many companies, instead of using their own (orange) livery, they used the well proven red livery with the addition of familiar London names and features. *A. Morgan*

In May 1993, Routemaster Bournemouth commenced operations with the introduction of route 604. Former KCB RM357 is a typical example, having been re-registered for the second time since leaving London and repainted in this green and cream livery. *T. Wilson*

In April 1989 East Midlands was loaned former United Counties RM980. In July, it was joined by former Magicbus RM2063 and both were used on routes around Mansfield in competition with Maun Buses. By the end of the year, four former Magicbus RMs had been acquired. By late summer of 1990, the fleet of six Routemasters had been fully repainted, each in a different livery. In addition, they were used on services in connection with the Sheffield World Student Games in July 1991. However they were all withdrawn on 27th July, with all the East Midland Routemasters in service on that day on every possible route in the Mansfield area. RM909, 1397 and 2063 were sold privately and the others were transferred to Stagecoach Scotland.

A small revival occurred over Christmas 1991/92 when privately owned RM652 ran East Midland's Christmas Shopper 'Santa's Specials' on various routes. From 10th to 18th February 1992, RM980 was hired to Sheffield Omnibus. Privately owned RM10 saw service with Sheffield Omnibus in July 1992, and FPT603C (numbered RMF2809) in October 1992.

Other companies to have employed a Routemaster on trial include Blue Bus of Eccles, Highland and Fife Scottish, Provincial and Brighton & Hove.

The well known Essex dealer and operator Ensignbus acquired RM1549, a former Kent County Council playbus. After extensive rebuilding, they ran it occasionally between June and September 1990 in their blue and silver livery, before exporting it to Japan.

One former Verwood Routemaster, RMA11, was used by Routemaster Travel of Aylesbury (initially on a four-month trial) from 11th November 1989 to November 1991 on routes 5/5A from Aylesbury to Leighton Buzzard and Stewkley. However, a minibus replaced the RMA and it was sold to Green Rover in November 1991.

Green Rover, after having used RMA14 from the spring of 1990 for tours to rallies, operated various services in the Watford and Harlow areas from 28th July 1990. RMA11 joined the fleet in November 1991 and various other vehicles, including Nostalgiabus RMC1462, were hired in to cover for the non-availability of the RMAs. The company ceased trading on 10th January 1993 and the vehicles have remained in storage. RMA11 was fitted with a front blind box and was repainted into fleet livery but did not re-enter service.

Despite continual rumours of the conversion to one-person operation, the use of Routemasters on Cumberland Motor Services route 61 (Harraby East to Morton Park) in Carlisle continued until 19th December 1992, although RMs 713 and 875 continued in spasmodic use until the end of the year. As with the United Counties vehicles, these Stagecoach vehicles remained in non-corporate livery until after their eventual replacement.

Haven Coaches acquired former Clydeside Scottish RMs 933 and 960, via Blue Triangle of Rainham, to operate in the Brighton and Newhaven area in competition with Brighton & Hove and Southdown from 29th July 1991. Both vehicles were repainted blue and silver, which is reminiscent of the former Ensignbus livery. RM960 was withdrawn and sold in the summer of 1992 and RM933 only made occasional appearances in service after this time. However, Haven Coaches was taken over by Blue Triangle from 16th January 1994.

North Mymms Coaches operated Leyland engined RM1975 and AEC engined RMA52 on services around Hatfield and in connection with the then new Galleria shopping centre from 1990 to 1992. RMA52 was fitted with a standard RM front blind box for these services. Former training vehicle RMC1500 was acquired direct from London Buses in March 1992 and was completely renovated and entered service in September 1992. RMA52 passed to Time Travel in August 1992. Former Northern General RMF RCN701 was acquired in October 1992 and later also passed to Time Travel.

Following the competition with Thamesway in the Southend area from 1991, Southend Transport became part of the British Bus Group from 1st June 1993. Up to the end of 1991, the Southend Transport Routemaster fleet had been expanded but withdrawals commenced from early 1993. All of the fleet was equipped with Transmatic fluorescent lighting and a refurbishment programme was commenced but never completed. Various DiPTAC features were fitted to these vehicles, including 'sharks-tooth' nosings to platform edges and yellow lower saloon grab rails. The last day of Routemaster operation was 31st December 1993 and on this day eight RMs together with RCL2256 were still operational.

In 1989, six Strathtay Scottish RMs (SR1-6) received Perth City Transport livery of deep red and cream for use on routes in Perth. This was in preparation for the Stagecoach 'Perth Panther' operation. In 1990, the fleet was rationalised, seven vehicles being sold and a further two being withdrawn for spares. With severe competition in Perth, the Routemaster operation was reduced in July 1991 and ceased altogether on 26th October after some five years operation. The remaining crew operations were now concentrated at Dundee. The six Perth City Transport liveried vehicles operated alongside the standard livered vehicles. In May 1992, Strathtay released two Routemaster registrations to preserved RMs 759 and 1691. The registrations had previously been transferred to other vehicles in the fleet. Throughout 1992 and 1993, the number of vehicles available for service gradually reduced. At the beginning of 1994, only RM26 was left with a valid certificate of fitness. Its last day of operation was 21st January 1994. Arbroath to Invergowrie (route 74) was the longest regular route then worked by a Routemaster in the United Kingdom (26 miles).

With Phase 3 of the introduction of the new Magic Minis at Corby (to continue the battle with the taxis), the United Counties Routemaster working in Corby ended altogether from 30th August 1991. The original Bedford operation started as a nine-month trial, but over five years later it was finally withdrawn on 4th September 1993.

Bellview Coaches of Paisley acquired former Strathtay RMs 298, 943 and 1017 and operated them on local services from October 1992 to January 1993.

Frontline acquired former KCB RMs 408 and 471 and from 5th March 1993 operated route 94 (Birmingham City Centre to Chelmsley Wood). Only the latter vehicle was used, but both vehicles were re-registered to KVS599 and 601 respectively. However the operation ceased within a month, but RM471 continued in use on a variety of duties until August 1994. Frontline became a part of the Badgerline group from August 1993. This was probably the only ever RM owned by this group. It even received new style (Badgerline) corporate seat moquette.

Midway of Greater Manchester (t/a Mancunian Buses) acquired nine former KCB and Strathtay Routemasters, including the vehicles from Bellview Coaches, primarily to operate route 143 (East Didsbury to Manchester Piccadilly) although they did operate various other contract and tendered services. Operations officially commenced on 30th March 1993 with a pvr of four RMs. They were repainted into London style red livery with a white relief. Of these, RM799 and 1017 were loaned to Cannon Coaches of Bolton during October and November 1993 respectively. Midway ceased trading from 11th February 1994, thereby ending RM operation in Manchester, yet again. All nine quickly passed to Blue Triangle in Essex and most have been re-sold.

Operational Routemasters returned to Bournemouth in 1993, after the demise of Verwood Transport in 1989. Routemaster Bournemouth acquired eleven RMs (ten former KCB and one former Clydeside example) although many others were loaned up to February 1994 (e.g. RMs 24, 621, 1959, 2156 and RMA37, although of these RMs 24 and 2156 were not used and RMA37 remained in its Verwood Transport livery). Most of the vehicles were repainted in a green and cream livery (including loaned RMs 621 and 1959) and re-registered in the series YVS 285 to 294 to match their new fleet numbers. Operations commenced from Easter and 17th May 1993 and ran to 10th August 1994. Officially Routemaster workings reduced over the winter of 1993, but there were still as many as five RMs regularly in service as they were by far the most reliable vehicles that the company operated. However, one single Routemaster, RM24, operated in passenger service in Bournemouth in 1995, trading as Route 24.

The ill-fated Darlington Transport recommenced crew operation on 24th May 1993, whilst in competition with South Durham, with the loan of East Yorkshire RM188 for approximately one week.

Clydeside 2000 re-commenced crew operation on the Glasgow to Paisley corridor from 23rd August 1993 with privately owned RM1975 and 2121 alongside resident RML900 and RMA16. However after a mutual agreement with Strathclyde, the operation ceased after 20th November. At the end of this operation, privately owned RM652, the first Clydeside Routemaster, had re-entered service with these others. It had re-gained its original registration and had been repainted in the Clydeside Scottish livery.

Early in 1994, the Hallamshire Bus company acquired former KCB RMs 367, 1145 and 1630. From late April, RM1145 was seen on route 277 (Sheffield to Doncaster via Meadowhall and Rotherham), but this operation had ceased in early July. The vehicles were subsequently sold, but an associate of this company acquired RM10, 1032 and FPT603C with the intention of introducing a new service early in 1995. However, Hallamshire surrendered their operator's licence and the service did not commence. From May 1995, Townbus of Poulton was operating FPT603C on a contract between a holiday camp in Lytham and Blackpool and also on route 53A (Poulton to Blackpool Airport). It was therefore the only Routemaster to work in Blackpool in 1995.

Five Iveco engined RMs were acquired from PVS by White Rose Coaches of Castleford. After repaint in a livery that was very similar to Reading Mainline, they entered service on route 164 (Leeds to Castleford) and peak hour variant X64, in competition with West Riding, from 12th December 1994 to 5th May 1995. The RMs were subsequently re-sold to PVS.

LONDON TRANSPORT BUSES

As BTS RML2443 awaits to turn into Regent Street on a hot June day, it shows off the standard features of the BTS RML fleet. Although these vehicles are leased from London Transport Buses, the radiator badges on the grilles were changed to read BTS. The vehicles are now fitted with Day-glo blind displays. *C. Lloyd*

BTS COACHES (part of Blazefield Holdings)

On 10th August 1993, the Tendered Bus Division of London Transport announced that the second crew route was to be operated by a private company with the result of the tender for route 13. Twenty-two Cummins engined RMLs were refurbished and repainted into full BTS livery of poppy red with a yellow band. Additionally a route diagram was applied to the advert panels. Internally they differed from other refurbished RMLs in that the exterior paintwork was continued around the platform and staircase area and also maroon paintwork was applied below the bench seats and in the luggage area in lieu of the standard LT red paintwork used on the red refurbished RMLs. The new operation commenced on 4th December 1993 and was based at the existing BTS depot in Borehamwood. The change of operator on route 13 saw the re-introduction of conductor operation and Routemasters on a Sunday in the capital. Former Southend Transport RM12 and RM104 were acquired from Martin's of Middlewich in March 1994. RM66 was acquired in April 1994, but for use as an Engineers Support vehicle. It was quickly repainted into full BTS livery and began life with another owner. RM104 was refurbished by BTS in the early summer of 1994, retaining its AEC engine and being completed in June. It entered service on route 13 on 11th July and is used as an additional spare vehicle. BTS Coaches were taken over by Blazefield Holdings from 5th August 1994. Former Southend Transport RM12 was finally cannibalised and scrapped in March 1995. Single-deck RM66 was sold to a Barnsley dealer in September 1995.

BTS Coaches operates RMLs on route 13 on behalf of London Transport Buses from Golders Green to Aldwych daily with a peak vehicle requirement (pvr) of 18.

CENTREWEST

CentreWest was sold to the management team on 2nd September 1994 and the fleet included four RMs, two RMCs and forty eight RMLs. All of the CentreWest RMLs, except RML2735, have Gold Arrow fleet names rather than CentreWest. RMs 944, 2103 and 2181 were subsequently sold in the summer of 1995 and RM1948 remained in passenger service until November 1995 and was then sold. The recruitment and training vehicle, RMC1492, was delicensed and stored at Westbourne Park in November 1995. RMC1510 underwent some minor refurbishment work in May and June 1993 including the fitment of a second hand Cummins engine (from the prototype vehicle RM2033), Transmatic fluorescent lighting to the lower deck, an interior repaint and re-trimming of the seats with the new RML-style moquette. The other five Cummins engined RMs were all withdrawn in the summer of 1992. A regular operation of the company is the use of Routemasters on midibus routes 28 and 31 over the Bank Holiday weekend of the Notting Hill Carnival.

All the RMLs in the CentreWest fleet are Cummins engined.

The following London Transport Buses routes are operated:

7	(Russell Square to East Acton Station) Westbourne Park garage	Mon-Sat	pvr 12
23	(Liverpool Street Station to Westbourne Park) Westbourne Park garage	Mon-Sat	pvr 29

CentreWest's RML2735 is the only RML in the fleet with CentreWest fleet names rather than the Gold Arrow ones. This vehicle was one of the prototype refurbishment vehicles in 1991 prior to the commencement of the RML refurbishment programme. It was subsequently added to the programme and brought up to the same standard in 1994. *M. King*

KENTISH BUS (part of British Bus Group)

On 9th December 1992, the Tendered Bus Division of London Transport announced the first crew route to be operated by a private company as the result of the tender for route 19. Twenty four Iveco engined RMLs were refurbished and repainted into a version of the full Kentish Bus livery of maroon and cream. For the first time a route diagram was applied to the advert panels. Internally they differed from other refurbished RMLs in that the platform and staircase area was painted burgundy in lieu of the standard LT red paintwork used on the red refurbished RMLs. Also, 'Welcome Aboard' was painted onto the platform Treadmaster and a timetable rack was fitted above the fire extinguisher on the staircase. The former quickly wore off and has not been replaced. The new operation commenced on 24th April 1993. As part of the contract, the RMLs are leased from LTB to Kentish Bus. About a week prior to the start of the new contract, Capital Citybus RM429 was borrowed from 16th to 23rd April to assist with the training of crews over the route as only RML2574 had been available for use by Kentish Bus. Major mechanical work on the RMLs is carried out at various other Kentish Bus premises including Walworth, Northfleet, Deptford and Ash Grove.

Kentish Bus moved their operational base on Sunday 13th October 1993 from the Nine Elms site at New Covent Garden SW8 to the annex and yard of the former LT Battersea garage in Hester Road. Kentish Bus RMLs have appeared on several other routes including special services for the Biggin Hill Air Fair and rallies at Sevenoaks. In the summer of 1993, the RMLs had the legend 'Part of the Proudmutual Transport Group' applied below their rear windows. However, after the group was taken over by British Bus in July 1994, this writing was slowly removed.

Kentish Bus operates RMLs on route 19 on behalf of London Transport Buses from Finsbury Park Station to Battersea Bridge (Hester Road) on Mondays to Saturdays with a pvr of 18.

Kentish Bus was the first private operator to commence an LT crew route in the capital.
RML2512 is seen in Piccadilly in July 1995. *Capital Transport*

LEASIDE BUSES (part of the Cowie Group plc)

Leaside Buses was sold to Cowie Group plc on 29th September 1994 and the fleet included one RM, one RMC and ninety four RMLs. From early 1995, the legend 'Cowie Group plc' was applied to all Routemasters above their rear platform window. Leaside became one of the first of the former London Buses companies to commence the removal and replacement of the London Buses triangles from the radiator grilles, using the Leaside swan instead. Cummins engined RML2408 was fitted in January 1995 with a particulate filter exhaust system and was the first Routemaster to be so fitted. RML2611 was also so fitted early in the summer of 1995. The tests to date have proved to be very successful and the equipment noticeably reduces exhaust smoke, fumes, smell and soot. RML2510 was fitted in early 1994 with a rear mounted roof aerial so that it could be 'tracked' by satellite whilst working on route 73. Leaside carried out the refurbishment of forty seven of their own RMLs between 1992 and 1994 as part of the London Buses RML refurbishment programme. In the summer of 1992, RMLs 2544 and 2588 were refurbished and retained their offside illuminated advert panels; they were re-wired and modernised with Transmatic equipment. These are the only two RMLs left with this equipment fitted. Leaside co-ordinated the supply of six RMLs for use at the Fifth International Amateur Athletic Federation World Athletic Competition in Gothenburg, Sweden between 1st and 14th August 1995 for use on courtesy services. The vehicles involved were Leaside's own RMLs 896 and 2758, CentreWest's RML2735, London Central's RML2283, Metroline's RML2431, and Stagecoach East London's RML2610. The two Leaside vehicles carried adverts on their roofs for the games. An additional vehicle was required for route 73 in October, and hence spare open top Iveco engined RMC1464 was used from sister company South London. It became officially transferred in December. RMC1453, numerically the first production RMC, was acquired by the company in August 1992 and has been undergoing a long term restoration since the summer of 1994, although at the time of writing, it was near to completion. Unlike Stagecoach East London's RMC1461, it has been repainted red. Despite the adoption of a new red livery with yellow stripes for the London Cowie operations, their Routemaster fleet is not being included in the current repaint programme. However, it will only be a matter of time before the fleet name of Cowie Leaside is applied to this fleet. Leaside Buses have won the 1996 LRPC award for the favourite crew route for route 73. All RMLs in the Leaside fleet are Cummins engined.

The following London Transport Buses routes are operated:

38 (Victoria Station to Clapton Pond)	Clapton garage	Mon-Sat	pvr 37
73 (Victoria Station to Stoke Newington Common)	Tottenham garage	Mon-Sat	pvr 47

Leaside Buses retained one RM, namely RM5. It is officially allocated to Clapton garage and when required it is used on route 38. However on 28th January 1994 it is seen on route 41 at Tottenham Hale station on the last day of Leaside operation of this route until it was regained in 1996. *M. Conway*

LONDON CENTRAL (part of the Go-Ahead Group plc)

London Central was sold to Go-Ahead Group plc on 22nd September 1994 and the fleet included forty six RMs and fifty eight RMLs. In February 1995, London Central's route 12 won the prestigious 1995 LRPC award in the best crew bus section of the annual competition which is awarded by votes from the travelling public for their favourite service on the basis of bus cleanliness, crew helpfulness and clear information displays. From December 1994, experimentation on five RMs took place to find a dedicated livery for route 36 vehicles. The livery on RM1104 was subsequently adopted for vehicles at Camberwell for route 12 as well as the mixed RM and RML allocation at New Cross for route 36. RMLs 2283 and 2613, both based at New Cross, are used for various special events and private hire work and are therefore not expected to receive this route branding. RM9 underwent some minor refurbishment in the spring of 1995, with the fitment of new RML refurbishment style fluorescent destination blind lighting and new flooring. It returned to passenger service in May following a full repaint. However, during July, it regained its original registration VLT9 from Stagecoach Selkent. RML2529 was returned to service in April 1995 after repair following major accident damage when the rear of the vehicle was demolished by South London Olympian L58 on 29th December 1994. It was repaired with the rear of the bodywork from RM1894. In the summer of 1995, minor refurbishment work commenced on the RM fleet for route 36. Fluorescent strip lighting has been fitted, ceilings have been painted and the interior side panels and seat backs have been re-trimmed. Following this programme, RM789 and 815 were withdrawn from service; the former providing the bodywork parts necessary to repair RML2499 after accident damage. RM71 is used as a training vehicle. A regular operation by the company is the use of Routemasters on routes 12, 12X and 36 on Bank Holidays and for the Notting Hill Carnival.

All RMLs in the London Central fleet are Cummins engined and the RMs remain AEC engined.

The following London Transport Buses routes are operated:

12 (Notting Hill Gate to Dulwich Plough)	Camberwell garage	Mon-Sat	pvr 38
36 (Queens Park Station to Lewisham)	New Cross garage	Mon-Sat	pvr 44

The RMLs at Camberwell are allocated to route 12 and, after the trials with the RMs on route 36, have had route branding applied. RML2733 is seen at Marble Arch in August 1995. *A. G. Izatt*

LONDON GENERAL

London General was sold to a MEBO team on 2nd November 1994 and the fleet included one RM and sixty eight RMLs. London General, along with Leaside, became the first of the former London Buses companies to commence the removal and replacement of the London Buses triangles from the radiator grilles with the 'B-type bus' logo instead. Following the privatisation, repaints started in the summer of 1995. The previous London Buses livery of all over red with white relief, grey 'dog' rail and black mudguards was retained but with the addition of new style London General fleet names on both sides and on the front roof dome. RML2403 was the first to be so treated in June.

RM994 was given a mini-refurbishment by Northern Counties in March 1992. RML2745 was converted to air brakes by Dennis Specialist Vehicles in February 1992 and remains unique. DRM2516 was re-registered to WLT516 in February 1994. RM994 was re-registered VLT89 in January 1994 but in December 1995 it regained its original registration. All Routemasters in the London General fleet are Iveco engined.

The following London Transport Buses routes are operated:

11 (Liverpool Street Station to Fulham Broadway)	Waterloo garage	Mon-Fri	pvr 20
14 (Putney Heath to Tottenham Court Road station)	Putney garage	Mon-Sat	pvr 21
22 (Putney Common to Piccadilly Circus)	Putney garage	Mon-Sat	pvr 15

London General adopted a new post-privatisation livery during 1995. So far only a few RMLs have been repainted. RML2403 was the first vehicle to appear with the new fleet names as well as the existing route branding. *C. Lloyd*

London General's DRM2516 was originally not to have been refurbished but in April 1993 it was completed and retained all of its unique features and embellishments. When not on special duties, it is to be seen on route 11 and was caught looking resplendent in Victoria in May 1995. *C. Lloyd*

LONDON UNITED

London United was sold to a MEBO team on 5th November 1994 and the fleet included one RMA, one RMC and thirty-nine RMLs. RMA55 re-joined RMC1469 on training duties from March 1995 but both were withdrawn by October and stored in Fulwell garage. The first Routemaster in this fleet to appear in a new post-privatisation livery was RML2349 in August 1995. The new livery featured a grey relief band, wheels, 'dog' rail, yellow fleet numbers, legal lettering and the additional fleet numbers added beneath the nearside rear tail light and nearside head lamp. The refurbishment of RML880 was completed in June 1993; it was again repainted in the Tramways style livery and numbered ER880.

All the RMLs in the London United fleet are Cummins engined.

The following London Transport Buses routes are operated:

9 (Hammersmith Bus Station to Aldwych)	Shepherds Bush garage	Mon-Sat	pvr 14
94 (Acton Green to Trafalgar Square)	Shepherds Bush garage	Mon-Sat	pvr 21

London United, in common with all of the other former London Buses operating companies, have selected a new livery and have started applying it to their RML fleet. However, owing to the LTB ruling that 80% of the vehicle should be red, only a very restrained version has appeared. RML2349 was the first vehicle to be outshopped after repaint.
G. Rixon

Since 1989, RML880 has been reclassified as ER880 and has carried the London United Tramways livery. It was refurbished in 1993, after being fitted with a Cummins engine, and retained its special colour scheme. *M. King*

METROLINE TRAVEL

Metroline was sold to a MEBO team on 7th October 1994 and the fleet included two RMs, one RMC and fifty RMLs. In July 1995, trials commenced to select a new livery for the RML fleet following the selection of the new all-over red livery with blue skirt for the opo fleet. Various different applications were applied to five vehicles, including the painting of the lower deck windows blue on RML2755, before the adoption of the final livery. The new livery for the RMLs was essentially the previous standard London Buses livery but with the addition of a thin blue skirt along the sides, a blue grille and new style Metroline fleet names with the addition of the legend 'To and from the West End'. Open-top RM644 was acquired in late 1991 and was the only former London Coaches open top Routemaster to have been used by another operator; all the others have been scrapped. It was fitted with an RMC style rear end during April 1993 but unusually with new air operated doors rather than the electrically operated type. RMC1513 joined the fleet in December 1993 and was repainted red with a cream relief band. It is used with the Contract Services fleet and carries the garage code CS to signify this allocation. Former training vehicle RM70 was withdrawn in the summer of 1995 and it has been retained for possible future use.

All RMLs in the Metroline fleet are Cummins engined.

The following London Transport Buses routes are operated:

6 (Aldwych to Kensal Rise Station)	Willesden garage	Mon-Sat	pvr 22
98 (Willesden to Holborn, Red Lion Square)	Willesden garage	Mon-Sat	pvr 21

The final livery selected by Metroline for their Routemaster fleet first appeared in the summer of 1995 and consisted of blue skirt, blue grille and new style fleet names. RML2431 is seen at Metroline's Willesden garage. *Ian Bell*

MTL LONDON

London Northern was sold to MTL Trust Holdings on 26th October 1994 and the fleet included twenty six RMs and nineteen RMLs. The unrefurbished AEC engined former showbus RML903 regained its offside route number blind box by the end of 1994. Early in 1995, following the trials with RMLs 2393 and 2620 in December 1994, a repaint programme commenced and all the RMLs, including RML903, were repainted into all-over red with the bold MTL London Northern fleet names. The last of the nineteen RMLs was completed in August. However a start on the RM fleet did not commence until November with the simultaneous omission of their RM code on their fleet number. RM1287 was withdrawn in October 1995 and subsequently cannibalised.

The RMLs in the MTL fleet are Cummins engined (except RML903 as noted above) and the RMs remain AEC engined.

The following London Transport Buses routes are operated:

10 (Hammersmith Bus Station to Archway Station)	Holloway garage	Mon-Sat	pvr 19
139 (Trafalgar Square to Golders Green Station)	Holloway garage	Mon-Sat	pvr 18

During 1995, all nineteen of MTL London's RMLs were repainted in the all-over red livery with MTL logos. On the nearside an MTL Trust Holdings logo was also placed. The RMLs are theoretically allocated to route 10 and RML2367 is seen on its way to Kings Cross in August 1995 at Marble Arch.
A. G. Izatt

MTL London commenced a repaint programme to their RM fleet during late 1995. RM1758, with the London Central style silver on black registration plate, displays the new livery, with no relief band and numbered 1758 rather than RM1758.
R. Knightley

SOUTH LONDON (part of the Cowie Group plc)

South London was sold to Cowie Group plc on 8th December 1994 and the fleet included thirty one RMs, one RMC and twenty seven RMLs. The sale had been delayed after problems with the Traffic Commissioner and hence the duration of their operator's licence had been cut immediately prior to the intended time of the sale of the company. All of the RMs, except RMs 311, 1125, 1725 and 2179, were repainted during 1994 into a dedicated livery for route 159 of red with cream lower and upper deck window surrounds and roof, with the addition of route diagrams along their advert panels. Additionally, all the RMs received fluorescent strip lighting, DiPTAC hand rails, 'shark-tooth' stair nosings and new rear light fittings. The new contract for route 159 commenced on 29th January 1994. RM1324 regained its original registration (324CLT) in April 1994. This was the first time that this had occurred in London. From early 1995, the legend 'Cowie Group plc' was applied to all Routemasters above their rear platform window. Surplus open top RMC1464 was loaned to Leaside in October and was officially transferred in December. As part of a five year trial to cut exhaust emissions, in association with London Transport Buses, RMs 6, 348, 432, 467, 970 and 1801 and RMLs 2264, 2324, 2333, 2351, 2375 and 2549 have all been fitted with oxidation catalysts from January 1996. Despite the adoption of a new red livery with yellow stripes for the London Cowie operations, the Routemaster fleet is not being included in the current repaint programme. The fleet name of Cowie South London is likely to be applied to this fleet.

All the Routemasters in the South London fleet are Iveco engined.

The following London Transport Buses routes are operated:

137 (Streatham Hill to Oxford Circus)	Brixton garage	Mon-Sat	pvr 22
159 (Baker Street Station to Streatham Garage)	Brixton garage	Mon-Sat	pvr 24

During 1994, the majority of the RMs required for South London's route 159 were repainted in this dedicated livery. A re-registered RM1361 is seen crossing Lambeth Bridge complete with the route diagrams along the side advert panels. *T. Wilson*

STAGECOACH EAST LONDON

East London was sold to Stagecoach Holdings on 6th September 1994 and the fleet included two RMs, two RMAs, three RMCs and fifty four RMLs. In November 1994, RML2610 was the first of the fleet to be repainted with cream relief band and gold Stagecoach East London fleet names. This livery was then adopted for all of the Routemaster fleet. RMC1461 underwent a major restoration in the summer of 1994 and made its début at the Routemaster 40 celebrations in full Green Line livery. It has been used for a variety of special uses since this time and even operates on route 15 occasionally. During 1994, all of the remaining RMCs with the East London fleet were repainted and only RMC1456 retained the red and gold livery as formerly carried by the Beckton Express RMC vehicles. RMC1485 was repainted in the February to red and cream livery – a red version of the Green Line livery. The final RML, 2760, is included within this fleet and was not included as part of the London Buses RML refurbishment programme. Hence it remains to the original specification with AEC engine and internal colour scheme. It was repainted in June 1993, retaining its 'showbus' style livery with a cream band; a livery not carried by this vehicle when new in 1968. RMC1485 completed a round Britain 'Bus-a-thon' between 22nd July and 1st August 1995 in aid of the Foundation for Children with Leukaemia. The vehicle carried advertisements for the various sponsors for the trip and a Stagecoach East London logo remains on the front roof dome as a remnant of this event. Similarly RML2610 carries a similar logo on the centre of the roof on the offside after its trip to Sweden in August 1995. No other Stagecoach East London vehicles have been given this feature. RM1527 is loaned from time to time to the BBC at Elstree television studios where it is used in the Eastenders television series. As part of a five-year trial, to cut exhaust emissions, in association with London Transport Buses, RML2462 and 2495 have been fitted with oxidation catalysts since January 1996.

All RMLs in the Stagecoach East London fleet at Upton Park (except RML2760) are Cummins engined and those at Bow are Iveco engined. The RMs, RMAs and RMCs remain AEC engined.

The following London Transport Buses routes are operated:

8 (Victoria Station to Bow Church)	Bow garage	Mon-Sat	pvr 22
15 (Paddington Station to East Ham)	Upton Park garage	Mon-Sat	pvr 26

Standard refurbished RML2462 shows off its newly-applied Stagecoach livery whilst operating on route 8 at Victoria in April 1995. All of the RMLs allocated to Bow for route 8 are Iveco engined, whereas those on route 15 at Upton Park (except RML2760) are Cummins engined.
C. Lloyd

Stagecoach East London have retained two RMs, the lowest numerically being RM613 which is maintained in immaculate condition complete in showbus style livery and bodywork fittings, as seen at Marble Arch in August 1995. *A. G Izatt*

Two RMAs continue in service with Stagecoach East London and are just as likely to be seen on route 15 as any other Routemaster from the Upton Park allocation. In June every year, they regularly take their turn in operating the services to the annual North Weald rally which RMA8 is seen approaching. *M. King*

Stagecoach East London's RMC1461 occasionally makes appearances on route 15 in its full Green Line livery. On 24th May 1995 it is seen at Monument plated up as running number 15. *M. Conway*

LONDON TRANSPORT BUSES RESERVE FLEET

The LTB Reserve fleet arrived at the Universitybus premises in Hatfield in early December 1994. This followed the successful tender by this company for the storage and maintenance of the fleet of Routemasters. All are standard AEC engined vehicles. The thirty vehicles were selected from the vehicles stored at Fulwell Bus Sales and included many of the vehicles that formed part of the strategic reserve fleet that acted as cover whilst the RMLs were away being refurbished. Some received repaints whilst others only received some bodywork repairs prior to them leaving London Transport premises. They are stored in securely guarded premises and are generally not accessible to the public. All are intended to be ready for operation at very short notice.

RM1428 was exhibited at a British Trade Fair in Denmark in June 1992. Unusually it returned to the British Isles and re-entered passenger service. RM2050 is a former London Coaches vehicle.

RM32	XYJ428	1005	ALC290A	1562	
264		1078	KGH925A	1676	
295		1081		1825	
324		1138		2021	
342	KFF277	1204		2033	
385		1205	XYJ429	2050	
659	KFF239	1214		2078	
736	XYJ418	1292	NVS485	2097	
966		1330	KGH975A	2173	
995		1428		2213	

Registrations are shown only where they differ from the original.

The London Transport Buses Reserve fleet is stored at University bus premises at Hatfield and the thirty Routemasters are rarely seen by the public. Although many of the vehicles gained new RML refurbishment style radiator grilles, RM1428 received a new badge but on the later style grille with the registration plate hanging from the radiator. *London Transport Buses*

LONDON SIGHTSEEING OPERATORS
LONDON COACHES (part of the Pullmans Group)

London Coaches currently have a fleet of one standard RM, two open-top RMs with disabled lifts, ten extended open-top ERMs, twelve open-top RMs (of which four are of convertible open-top configuration), ten convertible open-top RCLs and one closed top RCL. The sole standard RM is RM545 which was fitted with a DAF engine in April 1988. RMs 307 and 450 were rebuilt in 1988 to open-top configuration and also had wheelchair lifts built into their nearside, thus becoming O36/10RL + 4 wheelchairs. In 1990 ten open-top RMs were converted into ERMs by the insertion of an additional standard bay in the middle, thus becoming O44/32R. In the same year, two RCLs were converted to open-top, upseated on the upper deck only, becoming O40/27RD; and RMs 313 and 398 received RMC-type rear ends complete with platform doors and became O36/28RD. At the end of 1990 and during 1991, RMs 313, 398, 479 and 710 were rebuilt to convertible open-top configuration, and the two of these vehicles that had not previously been fitted with RMC-type rear ends with platform doors were rebuilt accordingly. Thus RMs 313 and 398 became CO36/26RD and RMs 479 and 710 became CO36/28RD. The difference in the lower-deck seating capacity was that the two earlier vehicles were fitted with tape equipment in 1990. The 11-strong RCL class received new platform doors in 1987, and as secure rather than open-platform vehicles, they were the ideal choice for the fitment of tape equipment in 1990. Ten of the RCL class (RCL2260, numerically the last built, being the exception) were also rebuilt to convertible open top configuration during late 1990 and the first half of 1991. Hence the RCL class is believed to be as follows:

RCL 2220, 2245	CO40/27RD + tape equipment
RCL 2240, 2241, 2253, 2259	CO36/27RD + tape equipment
RCL 2235, 2243, 2248, 2250	CO36/29RD
RCL 2260	H36/29RD

For the commencement of the London Plus service in August 1991, eight of the ten ERMs were repainted in the new London Plus livery of red and cream. This livery was subsequently adopted for the sightseeing fleet. By the early summer of 1993 all vehicles had been repainted with the exception of RMs 307, 450, 545 and RCL2260.

London Coaches was the first of the London Buses operating subsidiaries to be privatised on 18th May 1992 when it was sold to its management. The main sightseeing operation was renamed the Original London Sightseeing Tour (i.e. deleting the word Transport). The fleet names, advertisements, blinds and radiator grille badges were all altered accordingly. From July 1992, five RCLs were repainted in all over advertisements for McDonalds. These were the first RCLs ever to be all-over advert buses. In August 1993, the RCLs had their all-over adverts removed, but this left a mucky orange livery. In late July 1993, all six RMAs had been advertised for sale. The first, RMA 65, was sold in November 1993. The remaining five RMAs were sold to Blue Triangle at Rainham in October 1994. Three quickly found new owners in Ireland. Early in 1994, the remaining RCLs were repainted from the remnants of the McDonalds all-over advert livery and RM545 and RCL2260 were repainted red, albeit a slightly darker shade than standard.

RM307 has been overseas several times and most recently visited Utrecht in the Netherlands in January 1995. ERM235 was repainted into an all-over advert for the Disney Satellite Television channel and re-entered service in early October 1995. As such it is the first ERM to carry an all-over advertisement livery. RCL 2250 appeared in an all-over advert for Planet Hollywood in March 1996.

ERM 80	90	143	235	242
84	94	163	237	281
RM307	428	479	710	1783
313	438	545	752	1864
398	450	704	753	1919
RCL 2220	2241	2245	2250	2259
2235	2243	2248	2253	2260
2240				

RM753 is one of the eleven permanent open-top RMs in the fleet which remain with open platforms. They continue in service on sightseeing duties.
C. Lloyd

Ten out of the eleven RCLs were rebuilt in 1990/91 to convertible open-top configuration. After their conversion for use by London Transport in 1980 the platforms had remained open until new doors were fitted in 1987.
A. Conway

In 1988, RMs 307 and 450 were converted to open top and rebuilt with wheelchair lifts in the nearside. The former is seen at the Routemaster 40 celebrations beside sister vehicle RM308.
P. Stephenson

All ten ERMs continue in regular service with London Coaches. ERM90 is seen with a good number of passengers in Victoria and illustrates the plain red painted grille with the removal of all LT associated items of trim. *M King*

In the autumn of 1995, ERM235 was repainted in to an all-over advertisement livery for the Disney Satellite channel. It still retained its front poster to signify which service it was working. *S Madden*

BIG BUS COMPANY

The Big Bus Company commenced operating former Blue Triangle open top FPT588C on sightseeing work in the capital from April 1992 onwards. It had been repainted in their maroon and cream livery and had its front blind box removed and panelled over. FPT592C was acquired in February 1995 and, after repaint in September, entered service in November 1995. Unlike FPT588C, the front blind box remains intact and in use. Former Cadbury's 'Stroller' liveried RM272 was acquired in October 1995 and entered service in February 1996. In January 1996, RM10 and FPT603C were acquired for future use.

RM10	XFF 258	
RM272	LDS 236A	numbered as RM236
	FPT 588C	numbered as RMF588
	FPT 592C	numbered as RMF592
	FPT 603C	

Open top former Northern General FPT588C has operated on The Big Bus Company sightseeing tours since March 1992. It had previously operated with Blue Triangle on their sightseeing tours. *T. Wilson*

Above The Big Bus Company acquired former Clydeside Scottish RM272 in late 1995 and it entered service on sightseeing duties in February 1996 numbered RM236 to match the registration numbers. *R. Upcraft*

During the Summer of 1995, front-entrance FPT592C was repainted in The Big Bus Company livery and prepared for use on the sightseeing tours in the winter. This former preserved vehicle had only the previous year been returned to the road after a lengthy restoration. *A. Morgan*

OTHER OWNERS
A I A TRAVEL, Birkenhead

RM1101 was acquired from London Buses in September 1994 and was re-registered to KFF367 from KGH969A in October 1995. It is mainly used for school contracts to the Birkenhead Tram Museum at Pacific Road where it is garaged. It has remained in London red livery, with cream relief and London Transport fleet names.

RM1101   KFF367

BLACKPOOL TRANSPORT

Blackpool Transport acquired their first six Leyland-engined Routemasters direct from London Buses in April and May 1986. They were repainted in a superb red and white livery, which was fully lined-out as well. Although the present Blackpool Transport livery is green and white, the red and white version is actually based on the company's pre-war colour scheme. Routemasters fitted in well with the existing fleet which included a number of crew-operated Leyland PD3s. A second batch of six Leyland-engined vehicles arrived in April 1988, again purchased direct from London Buses, as a response to the 'Baby Blue' minibus service initiated by Fylde Borough Transport. A programme of DiPTAC enhancements commenced in 1991 with at least RMs 848, 879, 1627, 1650, 1735 and 1966 all receiving yellow platform grab stanchions. In addition, various vehicles were fitted with new front indicators of a more modern type. After December 1991, the Blackpool Routemaster fleet did not operate in the winter months. The Routemaster fleet has not been operated since 1994. The second batch was operated and were all repainted for this season. RM848 and 879 were repainted in all over advert liveries for Pontins, based on a white background, but with a standard liveried front ends.

Currently the Routemaster fleet remains stored with no foreseeable date of operation but there are no plans to sell the remaining 12 vehicles. The promenade service to the Pontin's holiday camp has been operated by open-top Leyland Atlanteans instead.

RM 848   fleet number 522
RM 879   fleet number 527
RM 1357   fleet number 528
RM 1583   fleet number 521
RM 1627   fleet number 523
RM 1640   fleet number 524
RM 1650   fleet number 525
RM 1735   fleet number 526
RM 1966   fleet number 529
RM 1989   fleet number 530
RM 2071   fleet number 531
RM 2089   fleet number 533

BLACK PRINCE COACHES

Black Prince acquired two former Clydeside Scottish Routemasters, RM441 in September 1990 and RM2208 in February 1991. Still in its former owners' livery, both worked on route X51 from Leeds to Morley, Mondays to Saturdays. RM441 was repainted in March 1992 into Black Prince's traditional red and yellow livery complete with gold lining. However, before these two vehicles arrived, two former Strathtay Scottish Routemasters, RMs 217 and 610, appeared in July and September 1990 respectively, but they were returned to the dealers Ripley's in the following November. RM2208 was sold for preservation in May 1993. RM441 was repainted again in the summer of 1995.

RM441   LDS341A

A1A of Birkenhead have used Iveco engined RM1101 on heritage type services in the Liverpool area. It is also available for private hire use.
R. L. Wilson

RM441 remains in occasional use with Black Prince and has seen use on route X51 between Leeds and Morley. It retains its name, Rudolph, as applied by Clydeside Scottish.
M. King

BLUEBIRD BUSES (part of Stagecoach Holdings Ltd.)

This fleet of Routemasters was transferred to Bluebird Buses from Stagecoach Scotland in October 1994. Stagecoach had been the first Scottish operator to purchase second-hand Routemasters in 1985. The vehicles currently operated are the operational remnants from the fleets of Magicbus, East Midland and United Counties. All operational vehicles are based at Perth and are painted in full Stagecoach corporate livery with Stagecoach fleet names and full blinds, except at the rear, where the apertures have been panelled over. This operation was introduced in Perth from 17th September 1990 on circular route 2 (City Centre to Letham to Tulloch to City Centre) which had previously been operated by minibuses. This route was in competition with Strathtay Scottish route 2. Four Routemasters were used from the existing fleet. The peak vehicle requirement (pvr) was increased to six from 23rd August 1993 with the conversion of route 1 to crew operation. RM1968 was renumbered from 616 to 606 in August 1995. Former Selkent RMC1490 was acquired by Stagecoach when Selkent was sold to Stagecoach Holdings on 6th September 1994. It was transferred from storage at Whitehaven to Perth in November 1994 for use as a back-up vehicle or private hire work but was not in the event used. It received fleet number 608 but retained LT red livery. All of this once Leyland Routemaster fleet is now AEC engined and based at Inveralmond. Six vehicles are currently still required to operate on Mondays to Saturdays on the Perth circular routes 1 and 2. However, this nowadays depends on the availability of conductors. All of the operational RMs were refurbished in 1994/5 with Transmatic lighting and retrimmed with Stagecoach corporate seating moquette. RM1607, the last example to be refurbished, is currently delicensed and along with RMC1490 has become part of the Stagecoach preserved fleet. Former Magicbus and KCB RMA50 was re-numbered 651 within the Stagecoach Scotland fleet in March 1994 and has been similarly retained for possible preservation.

RM560	fleet number 602 EDS50A
RM980	fleet number 605 USK625
RM1164	fleet number 603 NSG636A
RM1224	fleet number 601 UYJ654
RM1245	fleet number 614 LDS210A
RM1289	fleet number 609 XSL596A
RM1599	fleet number 604 YTS820A
RM1607	fleet number 607 LDS201A
RM1968	fleet number 606
RMA50	fleet number 651 NMY634E
RMC1490	fleet number 608

RM560 illustrates the current livery as carried by the Routemasters of the Stagecoach subsidiary, Bluebird, in Perth. Full Stagecoach livery has been applied to these vehicles, but noteworthy items include the tidy chrome surround in place on the radiator grille, with a home-made aluminium triangle in place of the LT triangle, and the additional advertising carried on the lower panels. *P. Stephenson*

All the Bluebird Routemasters have been refurbished with Transmatic fluorescent lighting and Stagecoach corporate seat moquette. However, the orange side panels may be bright but possibly not to everybody's taste! *A Morgan*

BLUEBIRD of Middleton

Bluebird of Middleton acquired RM1020 from PVS at Barnsley in November 1994, and it has not been used to date. However it is currently under restoration for future use.

RM1020   PVS830

BLUE TRIANGLE

Blue Triangle of Romford is another small firm which was owned and managed from the start by a group of enthusiasts. As the name suggests. most of their original vehicles were built by AEC. At various times they have operated RM, RMA, RMC, open top RMF and RCL types, as well as acting as dealers and selling-on several former Scottish Bus Group RMs and most of the former London Coaches RMAs. Their open top RMF was sold in March 1992 and their RMC is currently not operational. In January 1995, they acquired RML900 from Clydeside 2000, but to date have not operated this vehicle and it remains stored. RMA49 was repainted into their full livery and sign written for sightseeing work; returning to service in September 1992 and was numbered RMS49 in their fleet. RCL2239 continues in service, and was last repainted in December 1991, when it regained twin headlamps. It remained in their fleet livery of red and cream. In January 1992, Blue Triangle moved to their present base in Rainham, Essex. All vehicles are used on a variety of duties including private hire work, Essex County Council contracts and sightseeing work.

Blue Triangle took over Haven Coaches from 16th January 1994. Their Routemaster operation had ceased on 27th November 1993 when RM933 was withdrawn from service. However, it did not remain idle for long and was returned to service shortly after the takeover. Blue Triangle operated former KCB and Mancunian RM245 with their Haven Bus subsidiary at Brighton, primarily on routes H2 between Seaford and North Peacehaven and H5 Whitehawk to Churchill Square. RM799 operated on Blue Triangle route 204 between Loughton and Debden in the full London Buses style livery as previously used by Mancunian. RM245 initially operated alongside former Haven RM933. Both vehicles were former Clydeside examples re-united nearly 500 miles further south. They were withdrawn in July and October 1994 respectively. Another Routemaster to have been acquired and to have seen service in 1994 with this company was RMC1477. It remained in Green Line livery and is currently stored. A further sixteen Routemasters are owned and are stored for re-sale.

The operational Routemasters in the Blue Triangle fleet are:

RCL 2239   RMS 49

Former BEA32 is returned to service and is now numbered RMS49. It is primarily used on sightseeing duties and is seen at Tower Hill.
P. Stephenson

BYGONE TOURS

Bygone Tours of Headcorn in Kent occasionally use RM1677 on special duties. It has remained in LT red livery with the addition of white Bygone fleet names and signwriting for company advertising. The names of overseas countries painted on the bus are for the company's coach operation; the RM has not itself been abroad.

RM1677

RM1677 has been owned by ByGone Tours since May 1989 and has rarely been seen in London. However, at the Routemaster 40 celebrations in September 1994 it operated several journeys on special route 40R for the day. *A. Morgan collection*

CAPITAL CITYBUS

Capital Citybus use RM429 regularly on a variety of routes and contracts as a reserve vehicle mainly from their Dagenham depot. Capital Citybus's predecessor, Ensign Citybus, acquired it from Allco Passenger Vehicles in April 1991, very quickly painted it in their yellow and silver livery and re-registered it in June 1991. It had previously operated with Greater Manchester Buses and Rotherham & District. It was repainted again in September 1992, but in the Hong Kong style of yellow and red livery. It has been allocated fleet number 903, although this is not carried.

RM429   XMD81A

Former Greater Manchester Buses RM429 has operated with Capital Citybus since 1991 and in the summer of 1992 was repainted in this Hong Kong style livery. It is regularly seen in service and in October 1995 is seen on route 252. *P. Weston*

CARTER'S COACHES of Colchester

This company acquired RM113 in late 1994 and it was used from early January 1995 on the Ipswich to Diss corridor on Suffolk County Council tendered services 642/643 until 24th September 1995. It retained London Transport red livery. This operator also inspected RM727 during the period from April to July 1992, but it did not operate in passenger service.

RM113   LFF881

Carters of Colchester operated former preserved RM113 during 1995 on Suffolk County Council Sunday service 644. It is seen at Eye in June of that year. *P. Weston*

THE CHESTER BUS & BOAT COMPANY, Great Boughton

The Chester Bus & Boat Tour is a partnership between Acorn Travel and Bithell's Boats, and was was formed in February 1995 with tours commencing in April 1995 in competition with the existing Guide Friday operation. Open-top former London Buses RM625 and 1836 are operated all year round. They have been repainted into full London Buses style livery of all-over red with a white relief. They arrived from PVS at Barnsley in April and June 1995 respectively with the open-top conversions carried out by Wilkinson of Scarborough prior to entering service.

RM625   XYJ419   1836   EGF285B

RM 625 was the first Routemaster to enter service on the Chester Bus & Boat Tour. These were the first open top Routemasters to operate in the UK outside London. *T. Wilson*

Confidence Bus & Coach continue to use one Routemaster, namely Leyland engined RM655. It is seen at Oadby on a school contract in June 1992. *C. Holt*

CONFIDENCE BUS & COACH, Oadby

Confidence Bus & Coach Hire of Oadby still operate Leyland-engined RM655 in their fleet. It came to them direct from London Buses in August 1985 and was repainted in their black and grey livery complete with red lining. A second Leyland-engined Routemaster, RM621, was acquired in June 1986 but was sold in October 1990 after receiving severe accident damage. The remaining vehicle continues to be used on school contracts and services connected with Leicester University.

RM655   fleet number 15

EAST YORKSHIRE MOTOR SERVICES

East Yorkshire originally acquired seven Routemasters direct from London Buses in April 1988 for operation on routes 56 and 56A from 3rd May 1988. The fleet was repainted in the traditional and very attractive livery of indigo, primrose and white. The fleet continued to increase in size with the acquisition of a total of 19 vehicles for service and a further five for spares. RMs 757, 1741 and 1990 were initially repainted in the Scarborough & District livery of red and white for use in Scarborough. RM727 was the first of three RMs to be refurbished internally early in 1993 by SYT at Rotherham. From 28th February 1995, crew operation in Hull was revised. Some nine RMs were withdrawn to leave only the routes 56/56A along the Holderness Road. This further rationalisation of the routes between East Yorkshire and Stagecoach-owned Kingston-upon-Hull (KHCT) took place as the Routemasters had been too successful on the jointly operated routes 3 and 4 (the East Yorkshire crew buses were operating the route more quickly than the opo vehicles run by KHCT). However, Routemaster operation finally ceased on Saturday 13th August 1995 after some seven years of operation. This was ahead of the forthcoming Holderness Road Bus Priority Scheme and the proposed introduction of Smart cards with the eventual hope of matching the running times achieved by the RMs. The last ten RMs were initially to be stored as a reserve fleet, but at the time of writing, RM188 is to be retained in the East Yorkshire vintage vehicle fleet, the three refurbished RMs are being retained in store, and RMs 1010, 2065 and 2210 have been converted to open top for use by East Yorkshire.

RM188	fleet number 808	RM1010 †	fleet number 819 EDS221A
RM727 r	fleet number 817 LDS239A	RM1741w	fleet number 809 PAG809A
RM732 r	fleet number 801 NRH801A	RM2065 †	fleet number 812
RM798 r	fleet number 802 NRH802A	RM2210 †	fleet number 816

r   Refurbished   †   Open top   w   Withdrawn

When Liverline became part of North Western, RM1776 was given the fleet number 776 in this rather unusual, for a Routemaster, position. This former Greater Manchester RM is seen on the Liverpool gyratory still in its former livery albeit with a modified fleet name. *R.L. Wilson*

ENSIGNBUS, Rainham, Essex

Ensignbus acquired RM1102 from London Buses with the initial intention of operating it as part of their London Pride Sightseeing Vintage fleet. However, no work was commenced on the vehicle and it remains stored.

RM1102

EMS Bus & Coach, Greasby, Birkenhead

EMS acquired Iveco engined RM1528 (KGJ117A) from London Buses via PVS at Barnsley in October 1994 and it was used on route 79 (Birkenhead to Prenton) and 179 (Woodside Ferry to Prenton) until replaced by a former Blackburn Leyland Atlantean. It retains full London red livery.

RM1528   KGJ117A

LIVERLINE
(part of British Bus Group company, North Western)

Liverline acquired RM 1776 in October 1990. It had been used on various services including the docks/tourist service (route 30); the peak hour university service to the halls of residence (route 34); and Central bus station to Halewood and Garston (routes 38/39).

From 16th July 1993, Liverline became part of the North Western Group which was already part of British Bus Group and RM1776 was given fleet number 776. It remained in use mainly on services to and from the University Students Union to the Halls of residence. RM1776 was withdrawn in March 1995 and is currently stored at the Liverline premises in Bootle.

RM1776

LONDON&COUNTRY (part of British Bus Group)

RM1183 was collected from Southend Transport on 4th October 1993 by London&Country and operated from 5th to 22nd October on school route 418 in full Southend Transport livery but fully blinded. An additional vehicle had been requested by Surrey County Council and to satisfy this request the Routemaster was used instead of two Leyland Nationals. The Routemaster returned to passenger service on 27th November operating routes 406 and 408 up to Christmas. By now the white Southend Transport fleet names had been removed and black London&Country ones applied instead. Prior to Christmas 1993, RM1183 operated on routes 406 and 408 on four the consecutive Saturdays and route 418 on the week immediately prior to Christmas. Over the Christmas holiday period, it was repainted into full London&Country livery and received fleet number 4109. It was officially taken into stock in December 1993. RM1183 operated on routes 406, 408, 410, 414 and 473 in 1994, In addition RMC4 was used as a back-up vehicle when required as it had been relicensed as a psv from the end of July 1993. In the summer of 1992, RMC4 had been re-engined with the Leyland 0600 unit from the unique Tynesider (MCN30K). Kentish Bus RML2266 was loaned to London&Country for operation on route 410 on 25th September 1994 but it was not fitted with destination blinds for this route. RM1183 suffered mechanical problems at the end of 1994 and RMC4, along with RT3775, had to substitute. Subsequently for 1995, RM1183 was re-engined and repainted into Lincoln green livery. It also received a Transmatic Fibreshield front roof dome. It was allocated to routes 410 and 465. During May and June 1995, RMLs were again borrowed from sister British Bus company Kentish Bus to cover for the temporary absence of RM1183. This was the first time that full blind displays for the relevant routes had been carried. Owing to a vehicle shortage at Addlestone, RM1183 was used in November and December 1995 on a school contract. RMA16 was acquired from sister British Bus Group company, Clydeside 2000, in August 1995 and was repainted into a version of the early 1970s Green Line livery and prepared for service at Leatherhead garage. It also regained the twin headlights that it had lost in Scotland after accident damage. RMA16 had been named 'George the Routemaster' by Clydeside Scottish at the end of 1988. This name has been retained on the lower saloon front bulkhead.

RM1183   RMA16   RMC 4

RMC4 continues to see use with London&Country even though it approaches its own fortieth anniversary in a few years time. In May 1994, it is seen at East Grinstead on route 473. *R. Godfrey*

McGILLS BUS SERVICE, Barrhead

Iveco engined RM89 was acquired directly from London Buses in August 1994. It was quickly repainted into fleet livery of red and grey. It entered service on 17th August and was notable in retaining its Iveco engine. It was thus the first RM to operate outside London with an Iveco engine and was also the first RM to be sold from London Buses for passenger service in the United Kingdom since the batch was sold to Southend Transport in the autumn of 1988. It regularly sees service on route 1 (Auchenback to Paisley or Renfrew Ferry) and plans were to use it for an indefinite period to promote the Barrhead Centenary events. Initially the route number was carried but, in common with other McGills' routes, it no longer is. RM89 had previously been well known as one of the two 'General' liveried Routemasters at the inauguration of London General in April 1989.

RM 89   VYJ893

McGills of Barrhead were the first company outside London to operate an Iveco engined RM when they purchased RM89 in 1994. It is seen in Paisley in January 1995 on its regular route. *M. King*

MTL Merseyrider (part of MTL Holdings)

Blue Triangle of Bootle purchased RMA58 from Brakell Omnibus Sales in November 1991 and placed it in service in a very smart red, blue and cream livery in May 1992. RM1449 was acquired in August 1993 and, along with RMA58, was shipped to Sweden on an advertising contract for five months with resident RM1701 from Swebus at Lidingo. RM1449 had quickly been re-registered with its original registration that was already owned by the company. RM1449 has subsequently passed into preservation. Blue Triangle was acquired by MTL Trust Holdings in May 1994. Subsequently RMA58 was re-acquired by Mr D Forrest, its previous owner, and placed on long-term loan to the Merseyrider unit within MTL.

RMA58   NMY655E   fleet number 0655

NOSTALGIABUS

Nostalgiabus commenced in spring 1992 with private hire and tour work. Vehicles are operated from a base in Mitcham, including RMC1462 restored to original Green Line colours but with Nostalgiabus fleet names. At times the RMC is hired out to other operators, including Green Rover in 1992 and Timebus in November 1995, coincidentally for operation in the same town, Watford.

Between 1st May and 25th September 1994, Nostalgiabus operated route 693 from Morden Hall Garden Centre to Merton Abbey Mills. RMC1462 was loaned to London&Country in June and July 1995 to cover for the absent RM1183 for Sunday route 410. Conversely, RM121 is frequently hired from the LBPG at Cobham to assist with various private hire and school contracts.

RMC1462

READING MAINLINE (Greater Reading Omnibus Co. Ltd.)

Reading Mainline's operations commenced on 23rd July 1994 with route A (Turnham's Farm via Town Centre to Whitley Wood) which required a pvr of five vehicles. Initially former Southend Transport vehicles were licensed for service. Route B was introduced on 8th October 1994 with a pvr of three vehicles. It was initially a short working of route A. Route E (Tilehurst Triangle via the town centre to Addington) was introduced on 21st January 1995 with a pvr of three vehicles. Route H was introduced on 13th May 1995 (Caversham via the town centre to Cressingham Road). Route H was extended to Lower Earley on Monday to Friday peak hours and Saturdays from 2nd September 1995. Route E was extended from Tilehurst Triangle to Tilehurst 'Bear Inn' from 9th December 1995 and the frequency was doubled. All routes are in competition with Reading Buses. Standard features include the fitment of Day-glo destination blinds all round, including in the offside of RM172. Initially vehicles were acquired from Southend Transport and Strathtay Scottish but vehicles have been acquired from a variety of other sources. Seven former London Buses RMs were acquired from PVS at Barnsley in early 1995 and two RMs were acquired directly from East Yorkshire. There is an ongoing programme to prepare vehicles for service in advance of route changes and introductions. RM1653 was acquired for spares in October 1995. Former Strathtay Scottish RM316 re-gained its original registration in June 1995 and RM1859 was re-seated returning to use as a psv in September 1995 after use by St John's Ambulance for seven years. RM23 was re-registered again in July 1995, thereby losing its unique T suffix registration. Further interest with RM23 is that in 1978, its body (B1166) emerged from accident repair with plain upper deck front windows rather than the normal opening window units.

Former Strathtay Scottish RM45 was fitted with fluorescent lighting upstairs only from its days with London Buses as a radio trainer. Vehicles that had previously operated with Southend Transport are fitted with Transmatic fluorescent lighting. Leyland engines are fitted to RMs 621, 1653 and 1859. Reading Mainline is now the largest operator of Routemasters outside London.

RM 23	fleet number 23 JFO256	RM 931 u	fleet number 24 MFF580
RM 26 u	fleet number 28 XSL220A	RM 937	fleet number 5
RM 44	fleet number 7	RM 949	fleet number 3 XVS319
RM 45 u	fleet number 12 AST415A	RM 993	fleet number 2
RM 172	fleet number 10 WYJ857	RM 999	fleet number 15 WVS423
RM 180 u	fleet number 20 XVS830	RM 1017	fleet number 8 YTS973A
RM 191	fleet number 11 AST416A	RM 1018 u	fleet number 18 PVS828
RM 244	fleet number 19 XVS839	RM 1143 u	fleet number 13 WTS186A
RM 316	fleet number 14	RM 1653 sp	fleet number —
RM 577	fleet number 6	RM 1859	fleet number 17
RM 621	fleet number 16	RM 1948	fleet number 29
RM 790	fleet number 9	RM 1990	fleet number 25
RM 838	fleet number 22 XYJ440	RM 2011	fleet number 4
RM 871 u	fleet number 26 NRH803A	RM 2034	fleet number 1
RM 917 u	fleet number 27 WTS102A	RM 2201 u	fleet number 21

u   Unlicensed and currently being prepared for service   sp   For spares only

Former Strathtay RM316 re-acquired its original registration after entering service with Reading Mainline. It is seen on route H and the use of running numbers incorporating the route number can be seen. *R. Martin*

Former Southend Transport RM172, although having had its registration removed before arriving in Reading, continues to retain many original features. *R. Martin*

The following routes are operated:

Line A	Turnham's Farm to Whitley Wood	pvr 5
Line B	Tilehurst Triangle to Northumberland Avenue Community Centre	pvr 4
Line E	Tilehurst 'Bear Inn' to Addington Road/Erleigh Road	pvr 5
Line H	Hemdeen Road to Lower Earley	pvr 3

During 1995, RM24 operated in Bournemouth on a sightseeing tour as route 24. This vehicle had been a promotional vehicle with Combustion Engineering of Stevenage from 1987 to 1993 and was used to promote Reading Mainline in 1994. *T. Jones*

ROUTE 24

From Easter until late August 1995, RM24 was operated by a company trading as Route 24 twice a week on a sightseeing tour in the Bournemouth area. This Routemaster has been restored to an immaculate condition and is also used on private hire work. It is due to re-enter service in May 1996.

ROUTEMASTER TRAVEL

Trading as Routemasters, this operator started new night route H29 from 24th April 1992 using RMs 1571 and 1959. The route operated on Friday and Saturday evenings and some Thursdays throughout the year. In addition, Routemaster Travel were involved in other services from time to time.

From 20th August 1992, the routeing of night route H29 was altered but from 29th October 1992 the timetable was altered and a second vehicle was required. RM2156 was purchased in November 1992 and the timetable was again altered after 5th December 1992. However route H29 ceased operation on 29th May 1993. RMA10 was re-licensed as a psv from August 1993, returning to service at the first Delaine running day. RM1571 and RMA10 remained active on private hire and contract work, the latter including British Rail and London Underground rail replacement work. During 1994 and 1995, vehicles were loaned to Mullaney's and Shire Coaches for use on their contract services. RMA10 was sold in February 1996 and RM1571 has been on long-term loan to Timebus since June 1995.

Routemaster Travel have operated the one-day, Christmas Day, route 715 in 1995, as in previous years since 1992, but along with RM1571 were Timebus vehicles RM2156 and RM2198. In 1994, Stagecoach East London RMC1461 operated on the route with RM1571 and the now sold 1959. CentreWest hired RM1571 and 1959 on New Years Eve 1994 for operation on route N89.

RM1571

SHAFTESBURY & DISTRICT

Routemaster operation became a part of this company after the ashes of Verwood Transport had settled. Based in the Dorset town of Motcombe, Shaftesbury & District operate local bus services, school transport and private hire work in the Shaftesbury and Salisbury areas with RMA37 in their fleet. This vehicle was acquired from the scrapyard of PVS at Barnsley in 1987 and consequently features various non-standard (to an RMA type vehicle) items e.g. opening front windscreen, canopy blind box, RMC type front blind box and, until fairly recently, non-opening front upper deck windows. A second former BEA Routemaster was acquired in March 1992 after lying dormant in the yard of Wombwell Diesels. It had been a training vehicle with London Buses and more recently owned by Clydeside/Western Scottish but rarely used. Currently it is being rebuilt for future use. RMA10 was acquired from Routemaster Travel in February 1996 for future use. Former Confidence RM621 was rebuilt by Shaftesbury & District during the winter of 1992/1993 and made its début at the Cobham gathering on 4th April 1993 before being repainted and placed on long term loan to Routemaster Bournemouth. It was subsequently sold to Reading Mainline in October 1994. Similarly RMC1477 was acquired in May 1993 and was rebuilt and restored to passenger service prior to sale to Blue Triangle in August 1994.

RMA10	NMY647E
RMA29	KGJ603D
RMA37	KGJ612D

RMA37 is still used by Shaftesbury & District in and around Shaftesbury and Salisbury. However, it is seen here in 1993 when it was loaned to Routemaster Bournemouth for use alongside their own former Scottish Routemasters. *A. G Izatt*

STAGECOACH HOLDINGS LTD (Reserve Fleet)

All of the Routemasters (except RMC1515 and RMs 528, 2060 and 2122) being held by Stagecoach were repainted into full Stagecoach corporate livery during early 1994. All of the former United Counties RMs are stored at Northampton (previously at Bedford) and all of the former Cumberland Motor Services RMs are stored at the former Whitehaven garage. These Stagecoach Cumberland and United Counties vehicles were re-tested in the spring of 1995 and 1996. However, on 2nd January 1996, RM51 was damaged by fire at the Northampton depot. Its future is now uncertain. RM2192 was again relicensed at the end of May 1995 for use at special events and on special services. It had similarly been licensed the previous summer in August and September 1994 primarily for the Delaine running day and the Routemaster 40 celebrations on 24th September. RM682 was stored at the South Coast Buses depot at Worthing in June and July 1994 but was not licensed for service. Stagecoach Selkent RMC1515, although officially still in stock in the London based fleet, is also stored at Whitehaven. RMC1515 was acquired by Stagecoach when Selkent was sold to Stagecoach Holdings on 6th September 1994 and was transferred to Whitehaven in the October. The other three RMs are stored on Ribble premises at Blackburn. They arrived in store at Blackburn in October 1992 for evaluation at Bolton for service M10 (Manchester to Brookhouse). Initially they remained in their former United Counties green livery, but were repainted all-over white. They have not seen passenger service with Ribble, although were regularly seen from time to time on various duties, and are now officially withdrawn for disposal.

RM 51	UC fleet number 709	HVS936	RM 1647	UC fleet number 706	BNK32A
RM 255	UC fleet number 710	HVS935	RM 1933	CMS fleet number 904	
RM 512	UC fleet number 701	HVS710	RM 1941	CMS fleet number 902	
RM 528		WSK219	RM 1983	CMS fleet number 903	
RM 682	UC fleet number 703	HVS937	RM 2024	CMS fleet number 901	
RM 706	CMS fleet number 905	TSK269	RM 2060		
RM 713	CMS fleet number 900	TSK270	RM 2122		
RM 824	CMS fleet number 907	TSK271	RM 2192	UC fleet number 708	
RM 875	CMS fleet number 906	OVS940	RMC 1515		
RM 1068	UC fleet number 705	ABD892A			

RMC1490 is not sure if it is a Stagecoach Perth vehicle or a Selkent Travel one. It now resides at the Scottish Bus Museum in Lathalmond as part of the Stagecoach preserved fleet. *P. Stephenson*

TIMEBUS TRAVEL

TIMEBUS TRAVEL commenced their first commercial service on 22nd March 1993 with the operation of route 74 in St Albans using former Burnley & Pendle RM2180. It had been repainted red with flake grey bands around the upstairs windows and below the lower deck windows as well in the standard central relief position. It was also downseated to H36/24R by the removal of the offside bench seat and its replacement by a luggage rack. However, the Routemaster was used on this route for only two weeks, being replaced by a minibus after 3rd April due to very poor patronage. This was not the end of the operation of this Routemaster as on the evening of 3rd April it operated on a rail replacement service from Harrow to Rickmansworth. The last day of operation of route 74 was 22nd May; the Routemaster was used on this final day. Operations in Watford commenced on 16th July 1994 with route 73 (initially only Woodside, Boundary Way to Watford Town Centre). Their second Routemaster, RM2156, was acquired in October 1994. In common with RM2180, it had previously operated with Burnley & Pendle. Additionally, it was also downseated, as have all the additionally acquired or long-term loaned vehicles. The Saturday only route 73 operation was doubled in frequency to half hourly from 26th November 1994 and introduced as an hourly Monday to Saturday service from 28th November 1994. Former preserved RM2198 became a back-up vehicle for route 73 from April 1995. The frequency of route 73 was increased to half hourly on Monday to Saturday from 17th July 1995 and a new route 74 (Abbots Langley to Watford Town Centre) was introduced at the same time. Routemaster Travel RM1571 was received on long term loan from the end of June 1995 so that four RMs were available for the pvr of three. A timetable change was introduced on 11th November 1995 to both routes. Route 74 was increased in frequency to half-hourly all day Monday to Saturday and extended at the Abbots Langley end of the route so as to terminate at the same point as route 73. Route 73 was introduced on a Sunday, albeit primarily with RF operation. At the end of 1995, several vehicles were loaned to Timebus to cover for vehicles away undergoing various work, e.g. in November Nostalgiabus RMC1462 and in December London Bus Preservation Group's RM121 and BTS RM104 being used.

| RM1571 | RM2156 | RM2180 | RM2198 |

In July 1995 Timebus introduced a second route in North Watford and their original vehicle, RM2180, is seen at the Abbots Langley terminus soon afterwards. *R. Martin*

TIME TRAVEL, THORNTON HEATH

Former Northern General RCN701 was acquired in November 1992 and restored to psv operation in November 1994. Previously it had been a non-psv with Timothy Ashton Hospitality Buses of Epsom. Iveco engined RM1083 was acquired from London Buses via PVS at Barnsley (albeit collected directly from the former) in October 1994 and had platform doors fitted before entering service in the summer of 1995. Early in 1996, diaginal adverts for Carling Black Label were applied. Additionally, RMA57 has been used by this operator since the spring of 1995. RCN701 was numbered RMF2771 when acquired in 1980 by London Transport. The two RMAs are AEC engined and the RMF is Leyland engined.

RM1083	XVS850		RMA52	NMY637E
RMF2771	RCN701		RMA57	NMY654E

VILLAGE GROUP TOURS, Garston, Merseyside

Former KCB RM1630 was acquired from dealer J. Sykes in November 1994 and was repainted into London red livery. It was given fleet number V26 and used for private hire work. However, it did not remain in use for long and was placed in store in early 1995.

RM1630   EDS537B

VINTAGE YELLOW BUSES (part of Bournemouth Buses)

The Routemaster Bournemouth operation ceased trading after 10th August 1994. The Routemasters were reported as owned by Bournemouth Passenger Transport Association Limited (the Charity that owns the Bournemouth Bus Museum) and were hired out through the Association's trading company, Limpar Limited. An operator's licence in the name of Green Buses was obtained at the end of 1994 for the operation of buses in the Bournemouth area. However, following the mutual agreement between Green Buses Ltd, Bournemouth Transport Museum and Yellow Buses, Green Buses was renamed Vintage Yellow Buses and the livery of the former Bournemouth Corporation livery of primrose and maroon was adopted. Operations for the reformed company continue primarily on the well-known sea front and tourist services but vehicles are also seen on private hire and other contract work. In October 1995, RM219 was repainted into the fleet livery and re-entered service in this latter role. Additionally, it has operated on Yellow Buses football special route 86. RM809 has also been relicensed and sees occasional use although it remains in its old Routemaster Bournemouth green and cream livery. The other Routemaster vehicles remain stored at Hurn and are available for disposal. RM229 and 2083 were never in fact operated by Routemaster Bournemouth and retain their Kelvin Scottish Livery. The former is believed to still carry the registration EDS134A.

RM 55 w	fleet number 289	YVS289	RM 809	fleet number 286	YVS286
RM 219	fleet number 291	YVS291	RM 1134 w	fleet number 285	YVS285
RM 229 w	fleet number 294	YVS294	RM 1149 w	fleet number 290	YVS290
RM 357 w	fleet number 288	YVS288	RM 2083 w	fleet number 283	

w Withdrawn and in storage.

YORKSHIRE BELLES

The Yorkshire Belles Yesteryear Tour commenced from 2nd May 1994 as a niche sightseeing operation in York. Initially former Southend Transport RCL2256 was loaned from Brakell Omnibus Sales until the arrival of their own vehicle. RM388 arrived on 21st May and like the RCL was painted in an all-over maroon livery with a gold band. However, the RM has been unusually rebuilt by Kent Coachworks with an open rear staircase. RCL2256 was returned to Brakell in July 1994.

RM388   EDS300A

RMA52 has operated with North Mymms Coaches and more recently with Time Travel. However, in a rare appearance at a rally, it is seen at the Routemaster 40 celebrations at the Royal Victoria Docks in September 1994.
P. Stephenson

After a year following the withdrawal of the Routemaster Bournemouth operation, RM219 re-appeared in full Vintage Yellow Buses livery. Although the chrome surround to the radiator grille has been painted over, an RMA or RMF style triangle has been positioned.
A. Conway

In May 1994, a much modified former KCB RM388 re-entered service in York on sightseeing duties with Yorkshire Belles. It now has an open staircase following its conversion by Kent Coachworks. The tour of York with RM388 is a seasonal operation.
M. King

RM1166 has been owned by the Zoeftig Company Ltd in Bude, Cornwall, since February 1993 and has been used to promote their furniture. *V. Parsons*

NON-PSV USERS

With all types of double-deck bus, a certain percentage will always find new uses as publicity vehicles or hospitality units, mobile canteens or playbuses. The Routemaster is no exception, and the popularity of this bus has produced some unusual results. RM66, for example, was converted into a single deck towing vehicle and is actually preserved – but since the Routemaster is of chassisless construction, it is unlikely that it could ever be used in this role. RM110 is perhaps the ultimate show vehicle since it has been customised. It is now approximately two feet lower in height and has been fitted with a bar and juke box. However, it has not been seen at shows since 1993.

Conversion to open-top for promotional use is not uncommon, and RMs 238, 581 and 742 are used by local newspapers with this style of bodywork. Other promotional vehicles include RMs 87, 697, 843, 857, 1166, 2178 and RMC1496. Of these RM843 has appeared in two very distinctive liveries for Bravo Television, is strikingly trimmed internally and was due to be repainted again in 1996. RM1166 is probably more typical - with a bar fitted in the lower deck, most of the seats removed for display purposes and carpet fitted throughout. Conversely, only one standard RM, RM102 is used as a hospitality vehicle. In total four vehicles are currently used as playbuses and are RMs 1747, 1790, 1878 and RCL2218. Another non-PSV is RM216 which was extensively rebuilt as a project vehicle for GEC-Marconi Electronics and was fitted with many electronic items of equipment for its new role.

RM376 is used on several farms in Lincolnshire to transport workers. It was acquired to replace pre-war RT77. Former Magicbus RM831 has been used by Auto Recoveries as a turn-over vehicle at various shows in north west England. The London Transport Central Distribution Services (CDS) subsidiary at Acton own RCL2221 which is still available for hire. It is fitted out as an exhibition vehicle and was first used for the Shillibeer celebrations in 1979. RM811, a former CDS and London Coaches vehicle, was donated by London Transport to the David Shepherd Foundation on 26th July 1994 in exchange for a painting of a 1966 RML (with a pair of RTs and various contemporary vehicles) on Westminster Bridge. It is now used as a promotional vehicle for the foundation. During 1990, RM1159 was converted to open-top and re-fitted as a mobile fish bar. Similarly, RMC1495 has been converted into a roadside café. RM1643 is used by the Renal Unit at the Queen Elizabeth Hospital at Edgbaston to raise funds for their charities. Similarly, RM1767 is used by the Wing Fellowship Home for their charity work and is based at their West Bridgford Nottinghamshire base or at their Southport Lancashire base. Both of these buses have travelled abroad. RM1590 is also being prepared for similar such use. RM1262 is now in a multi-coloured livery as a mobile youth club and as such tours villages in East Anglia. RM1771 was originally part of the batch of vehicles that were to be scrapped by North's of Sherburn-in-Elmet after the first withdrawals in 1982. However, it survived, and has been used for a variety of uses including being hired to various companies to provide a bus service or for film work. Currently it is owned by a Night club in Doncaster. Former Rotherham & District and Greater Manchester Buses RM1807 was acquired by McDonalds Restaurants and is used as a Children's party bus in the Blackpool area. RM1842 has been converted into a mobile caravan and sees occasional use. RM2103 was one of the first Routemasters to be sold by a former London Buses company and in the autumn of 1995 was used on a 90-day tour around the United Kingdom undertaking work for the International Fund for Animal Welfare (IFAW). It is planned to continue on promotional work for the IFAW for the whole of 1996. This vehicle is owned by a company by the name of Freight Media. In early 1996, they acquired RM125, which is to be used by Mars to promote the Snickers chocolate bar in connection with their football sponsorship. It has been repainted in all-over green with football netting painted over the top. Internally it has been refitted to resemble a football pitch.

RCL2223 was extensively re-trimmed in 1986 at London Transport's Aldenham works and included the fitment of 22 coach-type seats and a kitchen area, and a downstairs bar. With its luxury fittings, it was used as both a hospitality and promotional vehicle. It was subsequently refitted with a demonstration area on the lower deck and the kitchen, conference and eating area on the upper deck. RCLs 2226 and 2238 have been used since their sale from London Buses as catering vehicles for the film industry. Former Magicbus RM1145 has also been used in this role since early 1995. RCL2254 is privately owned but was used by Bus Engineering Ltd (BEL) for promotional work until early 1993, and remains in a white livery.

Of the former Northern General vehicles, RCN689 has been used by Page Motors since 1979 as a promotional vehicle and is currently with their Poole office. Timothy Ashton Hospitality Buses of Epsom have been well known for owning several RMFs over the years, but no longer own any. The only other RMF in non-PSV use is FPT581C which is fitted out as a playbus but currently is for sale.

Surprisingly, not many of the former British Airways RMA vehicles have seen non-PSV use. As these vehicles are fitted with doors as standard (as with the RMFs), they would have been a natural choice for this type of work. RMAs 9 and 53 are available for hire as hospitality buses. The former is the former Wembley Stadium courtesy vehicle and has recently been refitted. The latter has been equipped with a bar upstairs and a display area downstairs. Externally it remains in London Transport red and has been fitted with an RM-type front blind box. RMA23 was used by Lever as a promotional vehicle, and had its staircase removed from the standard position and two staircases installed at the rear. However, it passed to an owner in the West Midlands area but has now disappeared. RMA62 is a playbus with the London Borough of Ealing and is now in its second livery with this owner.

Former Magicbus RM831, although currently out of use, has been used to demonstrate the recovery of turned over vehicles by Auto Recoveries of Carlisle. *Auto Recoveries*

In July 1994, RM811 was exchanged for a painting for the London Transport Museum. It now does valuable work for the David Shepherd Foundation, and is seen at Ingrow station. *P. Stephenson*

In 1994, RM843 was acquired by Bravo Timewarp Television and so far has appeared in two very distinctive liveries. The bus has been used for advertising work, at special events and with young children in a specially designed touring internet demonstration. However, it has recently been offered for sale. *P. Simmonds*

RM843 interior lower deck looking forward. The lower deck has been retrimmed with vortex walls and fake fur furnishings. This presentation suite has been used to show extracts from some of the Bravo Timewarp Television programmes. *Bravo*

For over ten years RM1767 has been used by the Winged Fellowship Trust. It is equipped with television and video equipment as well as shower, bedroom and kitchen facilities. Since the summer of 1995 it has been based in the London area. *G. Rixon*

Former Magicbus RM1145 is now used as Film location vehicle. *C. Lloyd*

RM1807 is used as a children's party bus by McDonald's near Blackpool. *D. Stewart*

RM1790 has been owned by the London Borough of Lewisham and used as a playbus since March 1985. Since this photograph was taken, it has been repainted and it remains in LBL style livery but with the addition of various different coloured balloons applied to the bodywork. *M. Conway*

The London Borough of Wandsworth still uses two Routemasters as playbuses. RM1878 makes a rare appearance at the gathering at Apps Court on the day of the Cobham Bus Museum open day in April 1995. *I. Norman*

During 1995, former CentreWest RM2103 undertook a tour of the British Isles as part of a campaign against the killing of Canadian seals. *T. Potter*

RM2178 was acquired by Pan Britannica Industries in 1993 and tours various events as The Bio Garden Bus to promote their products. *C. Lloyd*

The first RCL, 2218, is still used as a playbus with the London Borough of Redbridge. *P. Watson*

From 1994, RMC1495 has had a new role as 'Gus' the mobile catering vehicle. During the week it is used as a Café at Addlestone and at weekends it can be seen at various events. It is seen here at the 1995 Bus of Yesteryear Rally at Staines. *A. Morgan*

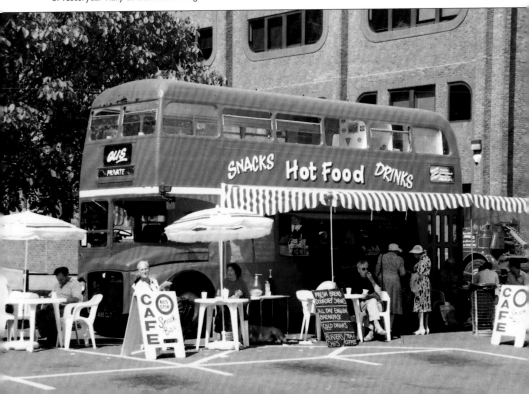

RCL2221 is still owned and used by the Central Distribution Services division of London Regional Transport. It is available for hire in its capacity as an exhibition and cinema bus, a role in which it was first used during the 1979 Shillibeer celebrations. *P. Stephenson*

RCL2223 continues in use as a luxury hospitality vehicle following its original conversion to this role at Aldenham works in 1984. *A. Cornish*

RCL2226 is now owned by Luna and continues in use as a catering vehicle for use on location by the film industry – a role, albeit with different owners, it has undertaken since 1985. *C. Lloyd*

RM216 makes very rare appearances on public roads and remains in use by GEC-Marconi Dynamics as a project vehicle. It normally remains out of sight within the secure premises in north London. *R. Martin*

Former London General Iveco engined RM1590 is currently owned by the Psychiatric Support & After-Care Workshops who are a charity organisation based at Ashford in Middlesex. It was repainted red in July 1995, having previously been in the London General livery. As with many non-psv vehicles it has had the platform rebuilt with a door. *D. C. Wilkinson*

Former Shillibeer RM2155 has been rebuilt with the Ashok engine and gearbox from a Leyland Comet. In April 1993 it is seen at Galle Face Green working from Maharagama depot on route 112 into Colombo. *A. Izatt*

OVERSEAS

It was only natural that the Routemaster would follow the RT class and be bought by overseas customers wanting to own a real London bus. It should be remembered that large numbers of double-deckers including Bristol FLFs and even Bristol VRs have been repainted red and shipped abroad and masquerade as London buses!

A one-off export was RML2691 for use by Mary Quant in Canada in 1972. Unfortunately, reports of this vehicle seem to have come to an end. It was last reported as travelling to Finland, but its whereabouts are now unknown.

From 1982, the London Buses vehicles became available and straight away four standard RMs were exported in August 1982 to the Karuizawa Classic Car Museum in Japan. Unusually, RM1248 was exported without an engine with the intention of being used as a static display. Since then, over two hundred and eighty RMs, two RCLs, eight RMCs and six RMAs have departed from the United Kingdom for 39 different countries around the world. The table opposite lists all of these countries and the number of vehicles known to be in each.

	RM	RML	RMA	RMC	RMF	RCL
Argentina	6					
Austria	1					
Australia	1					
Belgium	17				1	
Benin (West Africa)	1					
Canada	30					2
Czech Republic	1					
Denmark	2					
Finland	4	1			1	
France	15		3	5		
Germany	24			2		
Greece	1					
Hong Kong	3					
Hungary	8					
Ireland (Eire)	2		3			
Italy	5					
Japan	45					
Kenya	4					
Lebanon	1					
Luxembourg	1					
Mexico	3					
Netherlands	3					
New Zealand	3					
Norway	5					
Oman	1					
Paraguay	1					
Portugal	2					
Saudi Arabia	1					
Spain	10				1	
South Africa	2					
Sri Lanka	41					
Sweden	6			1		
Switzerland	2					
Turkey	2					
United Arab Emirates	1					
Uruguay	2					
USA	20					
(former) Yugoslavia	4					
Zimbabwe	1					
Total	282	1	6	8	3	2

Total number of Routemasters outside the UK: 302

The first other Routemasters to find owners abroad were two former Northern General RMFs (FPT589C and FPT591C) shipped to Spain in 1983 for promotional work and to Finland in 1984 as a hotel courtesy bus respectively.

Outside the UK, most are used for hospitality, promotional use or tourist services in one form or another with the exception of Sri Lanka. The Sri Lanka Transport Board acquired 41 Routemasters via the Crown Commissioner as part of an international aid package. However, at the last report, only five remained in regular passenger service. The main batch of 40 were exported in December 1988 following the acquisition of RM499 in 1985 and the many RT types in the 1950s. However, at least 75% are now withdrawn and are disused.

London Buses were hopeful for other orders during the 1980's but all came to nothing. There had been the possibility of a large number of Routemasters being exported to Japan for use as burger bars, but this fell through in 1989 and only small batches of them were exported there. Despite this, Japan now boasts the largest number of Routemasters outside the UK. Many of them have been used as mobile shops or restaurants, parked at various locations from time to time. Unfortunately, they were usually sold to an agent in the UK who sold them to a Japanese agent who in turn would pass them to their new owner. This system, together with the usual difficulties with the language barrier, resulted in very little information being returned to their homeland.

Operators in Canada were quick to acquire former London Buses Routemasters and currently Double Deck Tours at Niagara Falls own ten RMs and two RCLs, Piccadilly Bus Tours at Ottawa own six RMs, London Picadilly (yes, they do spell it this way) Buses at Tottenham own two RMs, Abegweit Tours in Charlottetown own two RMs, Royal Blue Line Tours own a former Burnley & Pendle RM and the Duke of Kent Bus Tours in Ontario own one RM all for tourist work. Finally, McDonalds Restaurants use RM1924, which is now at its second location, in Ontario as a children's party bus.

Six RMs operate on a sightseeing and tourist service for Beach Bus at Kittyhawk in North Carolina. Two further vehicles were initially purchased but have since passed to owners in Canada. Often vehicles employed on tourist services are used during the summer months only, i.e. June to August. One example of this type of seasonal work is RM2017 with the Chicago Motor Coach company. For this new role, it was fitted with an offside entrance and is open-top.

Twenty six Routemasters, including two RMCs, have gone to Germany. Again most have been put to use in various promotional roles including RM88 which is a mobile pub for Heidelberger. Other vehicles have also been converted into pseudo-British pubs. Routemasters are in many other European countries, and France now has fifteen RMs, five RMCs and three RMAs. Many of these are used on various tourist or promotional services. RM702 and open top RM339 are owned by The Imperial Red Ltd who are based in Toulouse. However, the company is also based in England at Worthing and both can be found in either country. In Sweden, RM192 is used to promote Lipton's tea. Of the five vehicles in Italy, RM1433 was converted to transport a motorcycle.

The Middle East is the home for four Routemasters. RM2171 and 2183 were shipped to Oman for a British Festival in 1989 and have found new owners in the area. RM521 was exported to Riyadh via the United Arab Emirates early in 1991 as a promotional vehicle for Mars Confectionery. The other vehicle, RM457, was exported to Beirut in 1985 for use by a fashion boutique but was last reported as being used to ferry guests between a palace and a race course in the Bekkaa Valley!

RM1708 is used as a school bus in Australia but is owned by a British family and is thus semi-preserved. In New Zealand, both RM1660 and 1670 are used for tourist services. RM1660 runs on a 50km round trip between Queenstown and Arrowtown in the Southern Lakes region of the Southern Island. Former Strathtay RM221 is owned by aviation enthusiast Sir Tim Wallis and is open top.

In 1983, De Dubbeldekkers based at Antwerp in Belgium acquired a number of RMs. However, most have since disappeared without trace. McDonalds Restaurants have acquired at least two RMs including former Clydeside Scottish RM924 which is visible from the Antwerp ring road. Additionally, there are at least three RMs for McDonalds in Germany.

Unfortunately, all contact with the four RMs in the former Yugoslavia has been lost and their current condition is unknown.

Africa is the home of eight Routemasters. Two are in South Africa and a third, RM1157, is in Benin outside a hotel as a static advert for cigarettes. It is in Sovereign King Size export livery of red with yellow vertical stripes. Another vehicle to be exported to this continent is former East Midland RM2063 which remains in its green and silver livery and is used to transport old age pensioners from Harare to Borrowdale village in Zimbabwe to receive free tea and scones at the owner's restaurant.

Perhaps the most bizarre adaptation of bodywork for a new use is in Hong Kong. In 1984, RMs 1288 and 1873 were exported in the hope that further orders would be forthcoming. In the late 1980's, they were rebuilt by Citybus but with wooden bodies, complete with wooden seats and open staircases in the approximate style of the London buses in the 1920's. The only recognisable features of these vehicles are the cabs and wheels! RM1288 is now in a pale blue and green livery, and numbered 1, while RM1873 is in a pale blue, cream and yellow livery and numbered 2. They primarily operate from the Star Ferry terminal to the Tram depot to connect with the tours of the tram system. In the summer of 1991, two further vehicles arrived in the Colony. One of these was former Clydeside Scottish RM1703 which is now open top and painted maroon. A fourth Routemaster, RM870, was not used and was later dismantled.

The most recent continent to see the influx of numerous Routemasters is South America with notably six RMs in Argentina and two RMs in Uruguay. The latter pair operate a free service at the resort of Punte del Este during the summer months of December to March. However, reports of the other vehicles are very sketchy.

Three RMs were exported by London Buses to Cancun in Mexico and are used to promote night clubs and a hotel. RM946 is static in Mexico City whilst RMs 735 and 2003 carry holiday makers from the Krystal Hotel and La Boom night club in Cancun on the Caribbean coast.

Former Southend Transport RM2005 and former London Coaches RMAs 25 and 26 are now operated by Dual Way Coaches on sightseeing services in Dublin. RMA25 was converted to open-top in 1995 and was the first RMA to be so converted. J J Kavanagh own former London Coaches RMA22 where it is used to operate on a $1^1/_2$ mile tour of Kilkenny, Ireland's smallest city.

Dual Way Coaches in Dublin operate three Routemasters on sightseeing work. Former Southampton City Transport and Southend Transport RM2005 was the first acquisition, followed by two former London Coaches RMAs. RMA25 was converted to open-top and became the first of the class ever to be converted. *R. Palmer*

RMA20 is seen near Lyon in September 1995 on promotional work. The addition of the blind box and the non-standard direction indicators are remnants from its previous owner Magicbus. *D. Chabaud*

The Sollac company in France own two RMs based at Dunkirk and RM611 based at Nantes. *A. Johnson*

RM98 is owned by SudbadenBus Gmbh in Freiburg in Germany and has had the platform and staircase reversed as well as being rebuilt with a lowered roof. *SudbadenBus*

Three Routemasters are used as children's play room and party buses outside various McDonalds restaurants in Germany. Former Southend Transport RM2101 is seen at Apolda, near Weimar in the former East Germany in September 1995. *A. Stokes*

Halden Traffikk in Norway own three RMs; RM549 and 1887 are currently operational and carry advertisements including on the latter over the windows. *Halden Traffikk*

RM720 is used as an exhibition unit for Apple Computers and in common with many Routemasters in Europe has had its roof cut down. In addition it is seen here with a trailer. *J. Pfiffner*

Bus Prophils in Belgium own part open top RM812 and raising roof RM1732. *Both photographs P. Roisin*

Beach Bus in Kitty Hawk own six Routemasters. They were acquired in early 1994 and included several former Southend Transport examples. One such example is RM1061 which was converted to open-top before export to the USA. *Beach Bus*

Former Northern FPT580C has been renovated and rebuilt as part open top. It is used on charter work by CreaMobil in Schoten in Belgium. A sign of the renovation work is the lack of beading in the usual places for a Routemaster on the sides of its Park Royal bodywork. *CreaMobil*

Both of the two Routemasters that were exported to Hong Kong in 1984 have been rebuilt to vintage style and are barely recognisable as Routemasters. RM1288, in its latest livery, is seen at Citybus Fo Tan depot in March 1996. *D. Stewart*

Former Clydeside Scottish RM1703 is the only Routemaster in Hong Kong which actually resembles how it left its manufacturers. However, it has now been converted to open-top and has lost its blind boxes. It is seen at the Star Ferry Terminal. *A. Conway*

RM730 is now owned by the Negombo Peopolised Transport Services; it is seen leaving the Negombo bus terminal. *G. Wright*

In 1985, RM499 was exported to Sri Lanka for evaluation. It was originally painted in Singapore Airlines livery but by April 1993, it had reverted to the red fleet livery. It is seen working on Ratmalana's route 102 at Galle Face Green. *A. Izatt*

Several Routemasters in Japan have had emergency offside exits fitted to both decks. Former Southampton City Transport RM1889 is one such example. *M. Bateman collection*

RM1889 on promotional duties. *W. O'Shea*

遊びながら、アジアを体験・体感。

ASIA PARK

アジアパーク

Two Routemasters are used on shuttle bus duties to the Asia Park at Kumamoto. RM1131 is seen at the terminus. *W. O'Shea*

Typical of the many Routemasters now in Japan, RM1384 is seen in Tokyo in its new role as a coffee shop. *P. Coney*

RM1187 was converted to open-top and had platform doors fitted before export to Japan in 1989. With its rebuilt bodywork it is used on sightseeing tours. *W. O'Shea*

Former Clydeside Scottish RM794 is covered with some 100,000 gold pennies and undertakes a tour past the Imax Theatre and the Skylon Tower at Niagara Falls. *R. Martin*

In 1995, Piccadilly Bus Tours of Ottawa converted two of their Routemasters to open-top. RM1773 is seen in their depot to the east of the city. *R. Martin*

Another former Piccadilly Bus Tours Routemaster is RM1448. It is now known as the Drury Lane Dairy Bar and is an ice cream parlour at the rather sinister sounding Experimental Farm on the south side of Toronto. *R. Martin*

Former Duke of Kent Tours RM1221 is now operated by the misspelt London Picadilly Buses of Tottenham (not to be confused with Piccadilly Bus Tours). It is used on a park-and-ride in connection with the preserved steam railway by the name of the South Simcoe Railway. *R. Martin*

The only two RCLs that have been exported are operated by Double Deck Tours of Niagara Falls. RCL2255 is fleet number 1 and has been owned since October 1983. *N. Eadon-Clarke*

Former Clydeside Scottish RM1152 is now preserved, but in June 1995 it was used at a wedding and is seen at Grindleton in Lancashire as the guests disembarked upon return from the church for the reception. *Pye's of Clitheroe*

PRESERVED

Being the last London designed traditional open rear platform bus, the popular Routemaster was a natural candidate for the preservationist. All four prototypes survive today. RMs 1 and 2 were donated to the London Transport Museum, Covent Garden, in March 1985, Leyland-engined RM3 was sold to the London Bus Preservation Trust at Cobham in February 1974 and Leyland-engined RMC4 passed to London&Country (then part of the Drawlane group) on privatisation in 1986. The unique front-entrance, rear engined Routemaster, FRM1, was donated to the London Transport Museum in May 1984. Of these none are on permanent display, and only RM2 was on display for a time when it was on long-term loan to the Oxford Bus Museum at Long Hanborough. RM1 makes rare appearances at rallies and FRM1 was PSV'd for the Routemaster 40 celebrations in 1994.

The number of Routemasters that have passed into preservation continues to increase every year and at early February 1996 (excluding the prototypes) there were 74 RMs, 7 RMCs, 6 RMAs, 4 RCLs and 4 RMFs currently preserved in one form or another in the United Kingdom. Of these RCL2229 and RM1737 were donated to the London Transport Museum in April 1985 and January 1986 respectively. Since December 1993, RM1737 has been on display at the London Transport Museum at Covent Garden. RM1737 is also famous as the first ever all-over advert bus when in August 1969 it appeared in a livery for Silexine Paints. Initially vehicles (excluding the RMFs) were sold directly from London Transport and included a few of the former garage showbuses (e.g. RMs 8, 254, 737, 1000 and 2116). Of these RM2116 is preserved in its '1933' livery that it gained in 1983 as part of the celebrations to commemorate fifty years of London Transport. RM8 saw only nine years service with London Transport, after use as an experimental vehicle based at Chiswick works. It was saved for preservation initially by a group from the now defunct Sidcup garage. As it is now approaching 14 years since sales commenced from London Transport, many buses have now had up to four or more owners. There are currently 17 Leyland-engined RMs preserved. Of the RMFs, only one retains a Leyland engine. Similarly, of the RMCs, prototype RMC4 retains a Leyland engine, being the only one of the class so fitted. In 1987, RM66 was cut down to a single-deck vehicle in a mock pseudo RM towing vehicle. Former Clydeside Scottish RM110 is now owned by a custom car club and has been fully customised as detailed in the non-psv chapter.

Museums with Routemasters in their collections include St Helens Museum with RM991 and RM1152, Sandtoft Trolleybus Museum with RM529, Aston Manor Road Transport Museum with RM506, the Greater Manchester Museum with RM1414, the Scottish Vintage Bus Museum with RM200, 371, 759 and numerous of the Stagecoach vintage fleet, and BaMMOT at Wythall with RCL2219. All of these vehicles are actually owned by individuals, with the exception of Stagecoach's and Greater Manchester's RM1414 which was donated by London Transport in January 1983. A former inhabitant of the St Helens Museum, RM460, was used by Pennine Blue at the end of 1993 as a publicity vehicle prior to the company being taken over by PMT and Badgerline.

Among all these vehicles, every example of London Transport livery is represented – except the current versions! In addition, four vehicles are currently preserved in the former Clydeside Scottish livery. Examples have been sold from Stagecoach and Strathtay Scottish for preservation, but they have all reverted to the colours of their original owners. One example is RM938 which attended the Bohemia Autofest in the Czech Republic in May 1992. Four former Southampton City Transport vehicles have been preserved but only two retain their second owner's livery. Only one of the former Southend Transport RMs (1543) retains its blue and white livery. In the autumn of 1995, RM548 joined the list of preserved vehicles and it retains the White Rose Coaches livery. Open-top RM1403, formerly owned by Allied Breweries, has retained its dark red Benskin's livery in preservation. This was the first RM converted to open-top configuration. RMs 54, 471 and 759 are currently preserved in liveries that Routemasters never actually carried in passenger service. RM54 was repainted in Blackburn Corporation Transport livery in early 1994 and RM471 was repainted in a version of the early post-war London Transport Country area Lincoln green and cream livery in early 1995. Former Strathtay RM759 was repainted in early 1993 to Glasgow Corporation livery complete with re-trimmed seats in DMS style London blue moquette and green paintwork in lieu of the burgundy rexine and gloss paintwork. Two of the RCLs that have been fully restored (i.e. RCLs 2219 and 2233) have been restored in the original Green Line livery, and of the preserved RMCs, four have been restored to original livery. The exceptions are RMC1459 which received the 1970's National Bus Company leaf green livery and RMC1476 which is restored as a London Buses 1980's training vehicle.

The former Northern General RMF fleet of fifty one vehicles has declined drastically. Only four vehicles are preserved, including the original RMF1254, which is slowly being restored to original as-built condition. From early 1992, Go-Ahead Northern have seen the occasional use of one of their original fleet of RMFs, former Stagecoach EDS508B (formerly RCN699), now re-registered PCN762. Although it has now been fitted with an AEC engine and has lost its original registration, one would not realise that it had left the fleet some 15 years previously. It is actually owned by the Go-Ahead Northern Bus Enthusiast Association and is used at shows and other special events. It was repainted in 1992 in a variation of its original livery of maroon and cream but with Northern fleet names.

The former British Airways RMA vehicles survive in reasonably large numbers with just over half of the class currently surviving. Two vehicles were restored to original BEA livery of mid-blue and white but of these only one remains preserved, this being BEA1 (otherwise remembered as RMA28). Additionally one was restored to the intermediate BEA livery of orange and white but this vehicle has since returned to PSV service with Time Travel. RMA6 is currently preserved in the BEL livery of grey and red. The others are preserved in London Transport red. RMA19 was rebuilt as a semi-preserved vehicle that could be used as a mobile caravan or hospitality vehicle, complete with shower and toilet. It has also been fitted with an RM type front blind box and over the last four years has seen use in a Children's television programme.

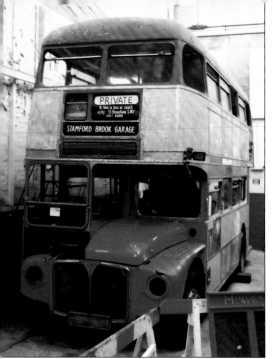

Above left In 1988 RM506 was donated to the Aston Manor Road Transport Museum from the West Midlands County Probation and After Care Service in a heavily vandalised condition. *A. Morgan*

Above right RMC1459 is the only preserved Routemaster which has been restored externally into the 1970s National Bus Company livery. Although it still has the RCL type radiator grille, it now has the RMC type headlamp panels either side with the brake cooling grilles correctly filled in. *A. Morgan*

RM471 was acquired by its present owner in October 1994 and repainted in this country area green livery. It is seen at one of its first appearances in April 1995 at Apps Court. *I. Norman*

RM2116 was one of four RMs to be painted in 1933 style liveries for the 50th Anniversary of LT in 1983. Although all four RMs survive, only RM2116 still carries the livery. It is seen at Quainton Road in July 1993 shortly after its most recent repaint. *A. Morgan*

In 1994, former Clydeside Scottish RM54 was repainted in the pre-war livery of Blackburn Corporation Transport. The significance of this livery is that Blackburn had two AEC Regent IIs delivered in 1939 which carried the fleet numbers 54 and 55. *M. King*

The only former White Rose Coaches RM to remain in the British Isles is RM548. It was acquired by its present owners in October 1995 for preservation. At the time of writing it is the only Iveco engined Routemaster to be preserved. *C. Suggitt*

A typical preserved Routemaster is RM642. It was acquired by its present owner in September 1991 and was restored to its original livery and near original condition – a nice touch is the lack of polished chrome additions although the radiator grille is the later type. *R. Martin*

RM1414 was donated by London Transport to the Museum of Transport in Manchester in 1983, some twenty years after its original loan to Manchester Corporation for assessment. *A. Morgan*

Another livery to be applied to a preserved RM is that of Glasgow Corporation Transport. Former Strathtay RM759 is seen with its original registration re-applied and demonstrating how well a Routemaster can look in a non-London livery. *P. Stephenson*

Every August Bank Holiday Saturday since 1993, there has been a very successful running day staged by Delaine of Bourne. Privately owned and former Southampton City Transport RM2059 was repainted for the first event and has operated on these days and at other events since then. *A. Morgan*

Former Clydeside Scottish and Black Prince RM2208 was restored to the 1979 Shillibeer livery for the Routemaster 40 celebration in September 1994. It is one of only four of the numerically correct Shillibeer vehicles to remain in existence and in the British Isles. *M. King*

Very few of the former Northern General RMFs still exist and only a few of these are preserved. Former Stevensons, Magicbus and Northern 2099 still holds a valid psv certificate and occasionally operates in passenger service. One such occasion was at the Routemaster 40 celebrations on 24th September 1994 when it operated on route 40R from the Royal Victoria Docks to Covent Garden. P. Weston

In the winter of 1990/91 former Northern 2133 was rebuilt with London style windows, blind boxes and seating moquette. It was then repainted in this London General style livery and re-numbered RMF2809. In September 1992 it became the first ever RMF type vehicle to operate in normal service in London when it operated on routes 111 and H23 for the London United Hounslow garage open day. A. Morgan

FRM1 has been part of the London Transport Museum collection since 1984 but in 1994 in was re-licensed as a psv for the Routemaster 40 celebration. From this date onwards it has made rare appearances at events and has occasionally carried passengers. It is seen at Canvey Island in October 1994 on the service from the rally to the Museum. A. Morgan

The only RMA to remain in the BEL grey livery is RMA6. It was sold for preservation in August 1987 and only started appearing at rallies from September 1994. *A. Morgan*

Every few years it is possible to pose the first Routemaster with the last Routemaster built. The prototype is seen with RML2760 at Canvey Island in October 1993. *A. Morgan*

ROUTEMASTERS IN EXISTENCE IN FEBRUARY 1996

Unlisted vehicles are believed to have been scrapped. All are AEC engined unless detailed.
Current re-registrations are shown where known.

RM

1	London Transport Museum (donated)	preserved, currently in storage
2	London Transport Museum (donated)	preserved, currently in storage
3	London Bus Preservation Trust, Cobham	preserved, Leyland engine
5	Leaside Buses - Clapton	
6	South London - Brixton	Iveco engine fitted 1991
7	Unknown owner, Doncaster	preserved but never rallied
8	RM8 Group, Sidcup	preserved
9	London Central - New Cross	
10	The Big Bus Co., London	re-reg XFF258 when preserved in 1995, under preparation for service
16	Messrs B Lewer & T Potter, Watford	preserved, Leyland engine
17	Mr A Harlott, Ipswich	re-reg WLT675 in 1994, preserved
18	South London - Brixton	Iveco engine fitted 1991
23	Reading Mainline (23)	re-reg JFO256 in 1995
24	Route 24, Bournemouth	preserved, occasional psv use
25	South London - Brixton	Iveco engine fitted 1991
26	Reading Mainline (28)	re-reg XSL220A by Strathtay Scottish in 1990, under preparation for service
29	MTL London - Holloway	re-reg OYM453A in 1988
32	London Transport Buses Reserve fleet - Hatfield	re-reg XYJ428 in 1994, in storage
40	RM40 Group, London E12	preserved
43	Mr J Kruining, Kooy Laminations BV, Aalsmeer, Netherlands	registered BE-16-50, open top
44	Reading Mainline (7)	Transmatic lighting fitted in 1992
45	Reading Mainline (12)	re-reg AST415A by Strathtay Scottish in 1988, fluorescent lighting fitted upstairs only, under preparation for service
47	Brakell Omnibus Sales (London) Ltd.	re-reg GVS492 by LBL in 1992
48	B Medni, Hayange, France	re-reg LDS199A by Western in 1989 Restaurant bus
51	Stagecoach United Counties (709) - Northampton	re-reg HVS936 in 1992, in storage, fire damaged 1996
53	Unknown owner, France	re-reg OYM582A by LBL in 1989, Iveco engine fitted 1991
54	Mr S Holmes, Blackburn	re-reg LDS279A by Western in 1990 preserved in Blackburn Corp. livery
55	Bournemouth Passenger Transport Association - Hurn	re-reg YVS289 in 1993, in storage
58	Le Museé de L'Auto, Le Mans, France	registered 9149-SQ-72
66	447 Group, Pontardawe, Swansea	preserved
70	Metroline - Cricklewood	converted to single-deck in 1987 withdrawn, former training vehicle
71	London Central - New Cross	trainer, re-reg UFF380 in 1995
80	London Coaches - Wandsworth	rebuilt & reclassified ERM in 1990
81	Cabriolet Cars, Funchal, Madeira, Portugal	re-reg LDS335A by Western in 1990, open top conversion 1996
83	Mr Z Keric, Yugoslavia	condition unknown
84	London Coaches - Wandsworth	rebuilt & reclassified ERM in 1990
85	Blue Triangle, Rainham, Essex	former promotional vehicle, for sale
87	Acamex Ltd, London	promotional vehicle
88	Heidelberg Pilsner Brewery, Germany	promotional vehicle re-reg OYM432A by LBL in 1988
89	McGills Bus Service, Barrhead	re-reg VYJ893 by LBL in 1994, Iveco engine fitted 1991
90	London Coaches - Wandsworth	rebuilt & reclassified ERM in 1990
94	London Coaches - Wandsworth	rebuilt & reclassified ERM in 1990

98	SudbadenBus Gmbh, Freiburg, Germany	registered FR JS 170, rebuilt with staircase on the nearside hospitality vehicle
102	DPR International, Bromley	re-reg LDS280A by Western in 1990
104	BTS Coaches, Borehamwood	refurbished by BTS in 1994
108	Mr I Lowings, Ascot	preserved, Leyland engine
109	Unisupply Co. Ltd., Kanagawa, Japan	Dining bus
110	Smoke City Wheelers, Tottenham	re-reg RSK572 in 1992, customised in 1992, Transmatic lighting fitted by Western in 1989
111	Blue Triangle, Rainham, Essex	in storage
113	Carters Coaches, East Burg Holt	re-reg LFF881 when preserved in 1994
116	Messrs T Nicholson & J Pye, Coulsdon	preserved, air suspension fitted by LT in 1980
120	London Bus Preservation Group, Cobham	open top
121	London Bus Preservation Group, Cobham	Leyland engine, occasional psv use
125	Freight Media, London	re-reg VVS373 by Allco Passenger Vehicles in 1993, being prepared for use as a promotional vehicle
140	Mr R C Gale, Avonwick	preserved
143	London Coaches - Wandsworth	rebuilt & reclassified ERM in 1990
149	Unknown owner, Germany	re-reg EDS117A by Kelvin Scottish in 1987
152	Sri Lanka Transport Board	registered 60 6613
154	Oliviera, Siracusa, Sicily, Italy	re-reg KGJ133A in 1992 in UK
158	Mr R Huckle, Sutton Coldfield	preserved
163	London Coaches - Wandsworth	rebuilt & reclassified ERM in 1990
172	Reading Mainline (10)	showbus, Transmatic lighting fitted by Southend Transport in 1988, re-reg WYJ857 by Southend Transport in 1993
180	Reading Mainline (20)	re-reg XVS830 by LBL in 1993 under preparation for service
187	Beach Bus Co., Kittyhawk, North Carolina, USA	Transmatic lighting fitted by Western in 1989, registered ZD3993
188	East Yorkshire (808) - Hull	stored as part of vintage vehicle fleet
191	Reading Mainline (11)	re-reg AST416A by Strathtay Scottish in 1988
192	Novia Livsmedelsindustries, Kristianstrad, Sweden	registered NMB576
194	Negombo Peopolised Transport Services, Negombo Sri Lanka	registered 60 6625
196	Mr D Brown, Muswell Hill	preserved
200	Messrs W Brydon & K Perrett, Cowdenbeath	preserved
202	London Central - New Cross	
204	Hontakasagoya Co. Ltd, Kobe, Japan	re-reg LDS233A by Western in 1990 Use unknown
206	Unknown owner, Gullegem, Belgium	re-reg LDS255A by Western in 1990
209	Fish and Chip shop, Vrasene, Belgium	registered ANV820
216	GEC-Marconi Dynamics Ltd., Stanmore	Project vehicle
219	Bournemouth Passenger Transport Association - Hurn	re-reg YVS291 in 1993, in storage Clydemaster refurbishment in 1989
221	Wanaka Lucern Ltd., Wanaka, Auckland, New Zealand	registered SD4295, open top
223	Exported to Norway	details unknown, re-reg WTS177A by Stagecoach in 1988
226	Mr Lionel Turcat, Martigues, France	re-reg LDS234A by Western in 1990 in use as a restaurant
229	Bournemouth Passenger Transport Association - Hurn	re-reg YVS294 in 1993, not operated in passenger service whilst with this owner, in storage
232	Telemark Sommarland, Telemark, Norway	
234	McDonalds Restaurants, Belgium	re-reg LDS235A by Western in 1990
235	London Coaches - Wandsworth	rebuilt & reclassified ERM in 1990
237	London Coaches - Wandsworth	rebuilt & reclassified ERM in 1990

238	Bucks Free Press, Amersham	open top promotional vehicle, named Henrietta
242	London Coaches - Wandsworth	rebuilt & reclassified ERM in 1990
244	Reading Mainline (19)	re-reg XVS839 by LBL in 1993
245	Blue Triangle, Rainham, Essex	re-reg LDS282A by Western in 1990, in storage
254	Mr G Rixon, East Molesey	preserved
255	Stagecoach United Counties (710) - Northampton	re-reg HVS935 in 1992, in storage
259	Brakell Omnibus Sales (London) Ltd.	
264	London Transport Buses Reserve fleet - Hatfield	in storage
268	MTL London - Holloway	
272	The Big Bus Co., London	re-reg LDS236A by Western in 1990
275	South London - Brixton	Iveco engine fitted 1993
281	London Coaches - Wandsworth	rebuilt & reclassified ERM in 1990
283	Negombo Peopolised Transport Services, Negombo, Sri Lanka	registered 60 6623
286	Discount Shop 31, Tokyo, Japan	Use unknown
291	Mr K McGowan, Rotherhithe	preserved
295	London Transport Buses Reserve fleet - Hatfield	in storage
298	Blue Triangle, Rainham, Essex	in storage, re-reg WTS245A by Strathtay Scottish in 1988
305	European Bus Centre (dealer), Bruges, Belgium	re-reg LDS256A by Western in 1990, current use and location unknown
307	London Coaches - Wandsworth	open top + wheelchair lift fitted 1988
308	Messrs A Morgan & K Saunders, London	preserved
311	South London - Brixton	Iveco engine fitted and re-reg KGJ142A in 1991
312	Exported to Tokyo, Japan	details of owner unknown
313	London Coaches - Wandsworth	convertible open top + doors fitted 1991
316	Reading Mainline (14)	
317	Punta Prava, Argentina	
318	R Barnham, Surrey, British Columbia, Canada	
321	Brakell Omnibus Sales (London) Ltd.	re-reg YTS824A by Kelvin Scottish in1987
324	London Transport Buses Reserve fleet - Hatfield	in storage
326	A C Brain Co. (3), Osaka, Japan	Leyland engine, offside emergency exits fitted, promotional vehicle
327	Negombo Peopolised Transport Services, Negombo, Sri Lanka	registered 60 6635
329	Scotts Minibuses, Hertford	re-reg MFF578 by LBL in 1994
333	Sri Lanka Transport Board (RL7)	registered 60 6612
335	T P S Technitube Rohrenwerke Gmbh, Duan, Germany	
339	Mrs C Vannier, Worthing	promotional vehicle in England and France; open top, re-reg MFF582 by LBL in 1994
342	London Transport Buses Reserve fleet - Hatfield	re-reg KFF277 in 1994, in storage
344	Sri Lanka Transport Board	registered 60 6636
346	Unknown owner	Iveco engine fitted in 1991, re-reg SVS615 by LBL in 1992, Location and use unknown
348	South London - Brixton	Iveco engine fitted 1990
349	Mr D Good, Croydon	preserved
354	Star & Liten AB, Stockholm, Sweden	registered MHN438
357	Bournemouth Passenger Transport Association - Hurn	re-reg YVS288 in 1993, in storage
359	Sollac Steel Works, Dunkirk, France	registered 6286-RX-59, named Jerry
364	Unknown owner	re-reg LDS337A by Western in 1990, Location and use unknown
371	Mr M Roulston, Glasgow	gold livery, named Golden Retriever, preserved
376	J W E Banks Ltd., Crowland	used on several farms
378	Mr P Stapleton, c/o Way Travel, Boreham	
385	London Transport Buses Reserve fleet - Hatfield	in storage

388	Yorkshire Belles, Haxby	rebuilt with open stair case in 1994
		re-reg EDS300A by Kelvin Scottish in 1988
395	L A Motor Coach Co., California, USA	Iveco engine fitted in 1991,
		re-reg VYJ892 by LBL in 1994,
398	London Coaches - Wandsworth	convertible open top + doors fitted 1991
406	Irish Commercials Ltd., Naas, Co. Kildare, Ireland	
408	Mr D Blackall, Ashford, Kent	preserved, re-reg KVS599 by Frontline in 1993
413	Mr Sisi, Carai SRL, Citta Di Castelo, Italy	
416	Unknown owner	re-reg LDS237A by Western in 1990
		Location and use unknown
421	Mr E Tapanines, Kuopio, Finland	Leyland engine
428	London Coaches - Wandsworth	open top conversion in 1986
429	Capital Citybus - Dagenham	re-reg XMD81A in 1991
432	South London - Brixton	re-reg SVS617 in 1992
		Iveco engine fitted in 1991
435	Sri Lanka Transport Board	registered 60 6620
436	London Central - New Cross	
438	London Coaches - Wandsworth	open top conversion in 1986
441	Black Prince Coaches, Morley	re-reg LDS341A by Western in 1990
		occasional psv use, named Rudolph
444	Mr R Jakob, Schweinfurt, Germany	re-reg LDS150A by Western in 1989
446	MTL London - Holloway	
447	Brakell Omnibus Sales (London) Ltd.	re-reg YVS293 and named Gerry by BHT Buses in 1993
450	London Coaches - Wandsworth	open top + wheelchair lift fitted 1988
457	Unknown Owner, Bekkaa Valley, Lebanon	
459	Unknown owner, France	
460	Mr J Worthington, Salford	preserved
467	South London - Brixton	re-reg XVS851 in 1993
		Iveco engine fitted 1990
470	Unknown owner, Dusseldorf, Germany	Iveco engine fitted 1991, Transmatic lighting fitted to lower deck in 1988, re-reg MFF504 by LBL in 1994
471	Mr R Dunkley, Croydon	preserved in green livery
		re-reg KVS601 by Frontline in 1993
478	London Central - New Cross	
479	London Coaches - Wandsworth	convertible open top + doors fitted 1991
494	last reported as with De Dubbeldekkers, Schilde, Belgium	Leyland engine, current location and use unknown
496	Kariuizawa Classic Car Museum, Nagano, Japan	Leyland engine
498	Bastad Buss Co., Bastad, Sweden	registered ECW313
499	Ratmanlana Peopolised Transport Services, Ratmanlana, Sri Lanka (RL11)	registered 60 2542, Leyland engine
504	Beach Bus Co., Kittyhawk, North Carolina, USA	open top, registered ZD3992
506	West Midlands Vintage Vehicle Society, Birmingham	preserved, Leyland engine
512	Stagecoach United Counties (701) - Northampton	re-reg HVS710 in 1992, in storage
516	Homegrown, Nairobi, Kenya	re-reg MFF518 by LBL in 1994, Use unknown
521	Mars Confectionery, Slough	exported to Riyadh, Saudi Arabia
525	Unknown owner, USA	Location and use unknown
527	London Central - New Cross	
528	Stagecoach Ribble - Blackburn	re-reg WSK219 by United Counties in 1992, in storage
529	Mr M Dare, Caversham	preserved
531	South London - Brixton	Iveco engine fitted 1990
541	London Central - New Cross	
545	London Coaches - Wandsworth	DAF engine fitted 1988
546	Brakell Omnibus Sales (London) Ltd.	re-reg LDS284A by Western in 1990
		Transmatic lighting fitted in 1991

548	Mr D Wilkinson, Staines	preserved, Iveco engine fitted in 1991, re-reg SVS618 by LBL in 1992
549	Halden Trafikk, Halden, Norway	registered AA29300, Leyland engine
550	Mr H Grimm, Play & Fun Gmbh, Plauen, Germany	re-reg LDS184A by Western in 1989, door fitted to platform, last reported at Ohrdruf
552	Octobus SARL, Paris, France	registered 586-JEW-75
555	Der Teelader Gbr Schwerlner, Borheim, Germany	
560	Bluebird Buses (602) - Perth	re-reg EDS50A in 1987,
564	Unknown owner, Tokyo, Japan	last reported at Midosiyi Boulevard as a wine bar, Leyland engine
577	Reading Mainline (6)	Transmatic lighting fitted by Southend Transport in 1988
581	Stephen Austin Newspapers, Hertford	open top conversion in 1985
583	Double Deck Tours (5), Niagara, Canada	registered BA4 846
584	The Company Bus, Winchcombe	for re-sale
592	Unknown owner, Japan	location and use unknown
596	Negombo Peopolised Transport Services, Negombo, Sri Lanka	registered 60 6632
597	Mr I Lowings, Ascot	
598	L A Motor Coach Co., California, USA	Iveco engine fitted in 1991, re-reg MFF510 by LBL in 1994
599	Tuckett Bros.	Iveco engine fitted 1991, re-reg MFF503 by LBL in 1994, location and use unknown
600	Mr Matsugi, Japan	location and use unknown
606	Unknown owner, Glasgow	preserved, re-reg EDS320A by Kelvin Scottish in1988, fluorescent lighting fitted in 1991
611	Sollac Steel Works, Nantes, France	registered 6295-RX-59, named Jerry
613	Stagecoach East London - Upton Park	
621	Reading Mainline (16)	Leyland engine
625	Chester Bus & Boat Co., Great Boughton, Chester	re-reg XYJ419 by LBL in 1994, open top conversion in 1995
626	London Bus Transport, Espoo, Finland	Operates sightseeing tours in Helsinki, registered NEL88, Leyland engine
632	McDonalds Restaurants, Tokyo, Japan	Party bus
638	Mitsui Greenland, Kumamoto, Japan	Asia Park shuttle bus
641	Mr Eistel, Menden, Germany	Hospitality vehicle
642	Mr P Simmonds, Morden	preserved
644	Metroline - Cricklewood	open top conversion 1988, doors fitted 1993
646	MTL London - Holloway	re-reg KFF257 in 1994
648	Unknown owner	re-reg XVS826 by LBL in 1993, Location and use unknown
649	Sri Lanka Transport Board	registered 60 6642
652	Mr G Watson, Chesterfield	preserved named 'Rodney the Routemaster'
654	Messrs M Begley & D Cartmill, Belfast	preserved, Leyland engine
655	Confidence Bus & Coach Hire(15), Oadby	Leyland engine
659	London Transport Buses Reserve fleet - Hatfield	re-reg KFF239 in 1994, in storage
663	Unknown owner, Quebec, Canada	registered A.11 963, door fitted to platform, undergoing conversion into a restaurant
664	South London - Brixton	Iveco engine fitted 1990
666	Messrs K Bevan, P Denham, C Sparkes, Newport, Gwent	preserved, re-reg WLT875 in 1993 and re-numbered RM875 in 1994
676	South London - Brixton	Iveco engine fitted 1991
682	Stagecoach United Counties (703) - Northampton	re-reg HVS937 in 1992, in storage
687	London Central - New Cross	
688	London Central - New Cross	
696	Exported to unknown owner	re-reg XVS829 by LBL in 1993, location and use unknown

697	Prestwold Estates, Prestwold	re-reg LDS238A by Western in 1990, hospitality vehicle
698	Decospray S.A., Buenos Aires, Argentina	
699	Mr S Bjork, Ljunskile, Sweden	registered PAN696
702	Mrs C Vannier, Worthing	promotional vehicle in England and France; re-reg WTS404A by Strathtay Scottish in 1988
704	London Coaches - Wandsworth	open top conversion in 1986
706	Stagecoach Cumberland (905) - Whitehaven	re-reg TSK269 in 1992, in storage
709	Hans-Grd, Vastert, Germany	
710	London Coaches - Wandsworth	convertible open top + doors fitted 1991
713	Stagecoach Cumberland (900) - Whitehaven	re-reg TSK270 in 1992, in storage
715	Unknown owner, Tokyo, Japan	
718	Roda British Transport & Promotions, Arnhem, Holland	registered BS-04-96
719	South London - Brixton	Iveco engine fitted 1993
720	Londag, Wadenswil, Switzerland	registered ZH-332-71U, exhibition unit for Apple Computers, fitted with canvas roof
727	East Yorkshire (817) - Hull	re-reg LDS239A by Western in 1990, refurbished by SYT in 1993, in storage
730	Negombo Peopolised Transport Services, Negombo, Sri Lanka	registered 60 6624
731	Sri Lanka Transport Board - Kandy	registered 60 6640
732	East Yorkshire (801) - Hull	re-reg NRH801A in 1990, refurbished by SYT in 1993, in storage
735	Senor I Vargas, Cancun, Mexico	Courtesy bus between The Krytsal Hotel and La Boom Night Club re-reg XYJ417 by LBL in 1994
736	London Transport Buses Reserve fleet - Hatfield	re-reg XYJ418 in 1994, in storage
737	RM737 Group, Harrow	preserved
742	York & County Press, York	promotional vehicle, part open top conversion in 1987
746	Sri Lanka Transport Board	registered 60 6611
751	Hafner-u-Fliesenlegergewerbe, Wilhelmsberg, Austria	re-reg KGH889A by LBL in 1991
752	London Coaches - Wandsworth	open top conversion in 1986
753	London Coaches - Wandsworth	open top conversion in 1988
757	Harrogate Eagles Venture Scouts, Harrogate	re-reg NVS855 by East Yorks in 1993
758	London Central - New Cross	
759	Mr M Roulston, Glasgow	preserved in Glasgow Corporation style livery
765	MTL London - Holloway	
769	Zadian SRL, Neroto Teramo, Italy	
775	Ringsted Energy Centre, Ringsted, Denmark	
781	Sollac Steel Works, Dunkirk, France	registered 6295-RX-59, named Tom
782	London Central - New Cross	
785	Shuzenji, Shizuoka, Japan	restaurant with air conditioning at Nijinosato theme park
787	London Central - New Cross	
788	Unknown owner, Hungary	roadside café between Kiskunfelegyhaza and Kistelek
789	London Central - New Cross	re-reg UFF389 in 1995, withdrawn
790	Reading Mainline (9)	
794	AA99 Inc., t/a Holiday VIP Tours, Niagara Falls, Canada	registered BF7 312, covered in old pennies and a 'Big Ben' in storage
795	Mr A Carr, Pluckley	
797	Beach Bus Co., Kittyhawk, North Carolina, USA	registered ZD4982, open top
798	East Yorkshire (802) - Hull	re-reg NRH802A in 1990, refurbished by SYT in 1993, in storage
799	Unknown owner	re-reg EDS312A by Kelvin Scottish in 1988, reported as exported.
800	Negombo Peopolised Transport Services, Negombo, Sri Lanka	registered 60 6628
804	Armitage, Barnsley	re-reg MFF581 by LBL in 1994

809	Bournemouth Passenger Transport Association - Hurn	re-reg YVS286 in 1993, in storage
811	David Shepherd Conservation Foundation - Preston	promotional vehicle
812	Mr P Roisin, Bus Prophils, Chatelet, Belgium	registered LAN558, part open top
815	London Central - New Cross	withdrawn, unregistered
820	Sakurai Ham, Kanagawa, Japan	Leyland engine, open top
822	Mr G Sibbons, Billericay	preserved
824	Stagecoach Cumberland (907) - Whitehaven	re-reg TSK271 in 1992, in storage
826	Unknown owner, Finland	re-reg KFF252 by LBL in 1994
828	Halden Trafikk, Halden, Norway	Leyland engine
831	Auto Recoveries, Carlisle	un-registered, turn-over vehicle
832	Unknown owner, Germany	re-reg BHU987A in 1991
835	Clydemaster Preservation Group, Brentwood	preserved
837	Exported to unknown owner	re-reg KGJ62A by LBL in 1991
838	Reading Mainline (22)	re-reg XYJ440 by LBL in 1994, under preparation for service
843	Bravo Timewarp Television, Watford	re-reg XVS828 by LBL in 1993
848	Blackpool Transport (522)	Leyland engine, Pontins all-over advert, in storage
851	Bus It, Tokyo, Japan	mens boutique
852	Sri Lanka Transport Board	registered 60 6610
857	South Park Motors, Reigate	promotional vehicle, Leyland engine
859	Mr Eeckhaut, Meulebeke, Belgium	re-reg LDS247A by Western in 1990, current use unknown
868	London Central - New Cross	
871	Reading Mainline (26)	re-reg NRH803A by East Yorkshire in 1991, under preparation for service
872	London Central - New Cross	
875	Stagecoach Cumberland (906) - Whitehaven	re-reg OVS940 in 1992, in storage
879	Blackpool Transport (527)	Leyland engine, in storage
905	Pepsi Cola, Istanbul, Turkey	promotional vehicle
909	Mr B Walker, Eastham	re-reg WTS418A by Stagecoach in 1988, preserved
910	Brakell Omnibus Sales (London) Ltd.	re-reg EDS288A by Kelvin Scottish in 1988
912	MTL London - Holloway	
917	Reading Mainline (27)	re-reg WTS102A by Strathtay Scottish in 1988, under preparation for service
918	Mr O Haack, Gotland, Sweden	registered NNY023, in use in Visby, rebuilt with offside exit
924	McDonalds Restaurants, Merksem, Belgium	re-reg LDS260A by Western in 1990, static childrens party bus
928	London Central - New Cross	
931	Reading Mainline (24)	re-reg MFF580 by LBL in 1994, under preparation for service
933	Blue Triangle, Rainham, Essex	in storage, Transmatic lighting fitted by Western in 1989
937	Reading Mainline (5)	Transmatic lighting fitted by Southend Transport in 1988
938	Mr I Hoskin, Mitcham	preserved
943	Blue Triangle, Rainham, Essex	in storage, re-reg WTS225A by Strathtay Scottish in 1988
944	Music Hall Theatre Co., Belgium	used as a mobile theatre, open top conversion in 1995
946	Senor I Vargas, Mexico City, Mexico	static display at a night club, open top, re-reg MFF577 by LBL in 1994
949	Reading Mainline (3)	re-reg XVS319 by Southend Transport in 1993, Transmatic lighting fitted by Southend Transport in 1988
951	Kangaroo International, Colnbrook	
956	The Company Bus, Winchcombe	re-reg LDS261A by Western in 1990, for re-sale
960	Mr A Gregory, Croydon	preserved
963	British American Bingo Inc., Washington, USA	For use at Muckleshoot Bingo Hall, Muckleshoot Indian Reserve, near Auburn

966	London Transport Buses Reserve fleet - Hatfield	in storage
967	London Central - New Cross	
969	London Bus Export Company, Chepstow	re-reg DFH806A in 1990, Leyland engine used for promotional work
970	South London - Brixton	Iveco engine fitted 1991
977	Maison Communale Des Jeunes, Huy, Belgium	For use by a youth club
978	Messrs A Harlott & A Brown, Romford	re-reg LDS164A by Western in1989
980	Bluebird Buses (605) - Perth	re-reg USK625 by East Midland in 1992
982	De Souza, Buenos Aires, Argentina	re-reg NVS804 by East Yorkshire in 1992, for use as a courtesy vehicle
985	Whiting Bros., Ferrybridge	partially scrapped
986	Unknown owner, Canada	registered BE9 683, Leyland engine, current use and condition unknown
991	Mr E Dickenson, Timperley	preserved
993	Reading Mainline (2)	Transmatic lighting fitted by Southend Transport in 1988
994	London General - Waterloo	refurbished by Northern Counties in 1992, Iveco engine fitted in 1991
995	London Transport Buses Reserve fleet - Hatfield	in storage
997	South London - Brixton	Iveco engine fitted in 1991
999	Reading Mainline(15)	re-reg WVS423 in 1994
1000	RM1000 Group, Croydon	preserved
1001	Mr M Smith, Billericay	preserved
1002	London Central - New Cross	re-reg OYM368A in 1987
1003	South London - Brixton	Iveco engine fitted in 1990
1005	London Transport Buses Reserve fleet - Hatfield	re-reg ALC290A in 1991, in storage
1006	Blue Triangle, Rainham, Essex	re-reg EDS98A by Kelvin Scottish in 1987, in storage
1009	Blue Triangle, Rainham, Essex	in storage
1010	East Yorkshire (819) - Hull	re-reg EDS221A by Kelvin Scottish in 1987, being converted to open-top
1013	Mr A Soucek, Prague, Czech Republic	re-reg LDS253A by Western in 1990
1017	Reading Mainline (8)	re-reg YTS973A by Strathtay Scottish in 1987
1018	Reading Mainline (18)	re-reg PVS828 by LBL in 1992, under preparation for service
1020	Bluebird, Middleton	re-reg PVS830 by LBL in 1992, under preparation for service
1026	Unknown owner, Spain	Leyland engine, location and use unknown
1029	Negombo Peopolised Transport Services, Negombo, Sri Lanka	registered 60 6626
1032	Mr G Pegg, Rotherham	re-reg YVS292 by BHT Buses in 1993, in storage
1033	London Central - New Cross	
1041	Brakell Omnibus Sales (London) Ltd.	re-reg NRH805A by East Yorkshire in 1990
1047	Mr O Vorlander, Ruppichferath, Germany	
1053	Mr R Conyers, West Moors	preserved, re-reg YVS287 by BHT Buses in 1993
1054	Rheinheimer Autoteile, Krickenback, Germany	re-reg LDS285A by Western in 1990
1058	London Central - New Cross	
1061	Beach Bus Co., Kittyhawk, North Carolina, USA	registered ZD3990, open top
1062	London Central - New Cross	
1063	Mr D Ladd, Richings Park	preserved
1067	Negombo Peopolised Transport Services, Negombo, Sri Lanka	registered 60 6633
1068	Stagecoach United Counties (705) - Northampton	re-reg ABD892A in 1991, in storage
1069	Mr D Sullivan, Harrow	preserved, occasional psv use
1070	Unknown owner	re-reg XYJ430 by LBL in 1994
1072	Mr G Kent, Ontario, Canada	t/a Duke of Kent Bus Tours, registered BH2 250
1077	Handelsbolaget Rode Orm, Mariehamm, Aland Is, Finland	re-reg KGH26A by Brakell in 1987, operates a tourist service
1078	London Transport Buses Reserve fleet - Hatfield	re-reg KGH925A in 1991, in storage

1080	Sri Lanka Transport Board	registered 60 6621
1081	London Transport Buses Reserve fleet - Hatfield	in storage
1082	London Central - New Cross	
1083	Time Travel -Thornton Heath	re-reg XVS850 by LBL in 1993, Iveco engine fitted in 1990, rear platform doors fitted in 1995
1086	Mr O Sejthen, Krussa, Denmark	
1087	Brakell Omnibus Sales (London) Ltd.	under conversion to open top
1088	Last reported with De Dubbeldekkers, Schilde, Belgium	current location and use unknown
1090	A C Brain Co., Osaka, Japan	offside emergency exits fitted, promotional vehicle, numbered as RM326
1097	London Central - New Cross	
1101	A1A Travel, Birkenhead	Iveco engine fitted in 1991, re-reg KFF367 in 1995
1102	Ensignbus, Rainham	in storage for possible future use
1104	London Central - New Cross	
1109	The Company Bus, Winchcombe	for re-sale
1111	Travellers Young Fashion, Augsburg, Germany	mobile clothes shop
1115	Ratmalana Peopolised Transport Services, Ratmanlana, Sri Lanka (RL13) registered 60 6609	
1117	Exported to Spain	unknown owner, Leyland engine
1119	London Central - New Cross	
1121	Sri Lanka Transport Board - Maharamgama	registered 60 6622
1123	Burton Biscuits, Blackpool	
1124	South London - Brixton	Iveco engine fitted and re-reg VYJ806 in 1993
1125	South London - Brixton	Iveco engine fitted in 1991, re-reg KGH858A in 1990
1131	Mitsui Greenland, Kumamoto, Japan	Asia Park shuttle bus
1133	Unknown owner, France	re-reg KFF240 by LBL in 1994
1134	Bournemouth Passenger Transport Association - Hurn	re-reg YVS285 in 1993, in storage
1136	Unknown owner, Buenos Aires, Argentina	
1138	London Transport Buses Reserve fleet - Hatfield	in storage
1143	Reading Mainline (13)	re-reg WTS186A by Strathtay Scottish in 1988, under preparation for service
1145	GT Transport, Borehamwood	film location vehicle re-reg LDS402A by Stagecoach in 1990
1149	Bournemouth Passenger Transport Association - Hurn	re-reg YVS290 in 1993, in storage
1150	Sri Lanka Transport Board	registered 60 6619
1152	Mr J Pryer, Sandbach	preserved
1154	Nichioh Trade Services, Kobe, Japan	location and use unknown
1156	Unknown owner, Netherlands	location and use unknown
1157	Sopexci, Benin, West Africa	static promotional vehicle
1158	MTL London - Holloway	
1159	Mr N Goodman, Herne Bay	Mobile fish restaurant, open top Leyland engine
1160	Sri Lanka Transport Board	registered 60 6631
1163	Last reported as with De Dubbeldekkers, Antwerp, Belgium	current location and use unknown, last reported at Schilde, Leyland engine
1164	Bluebird Buses (603) - Perth	re-reg NSG636A by East Midland in 1989
1165	Sri Lanka Transport Board	registered 60 6641
1166	Zoeftig & Co. Ltd., Bude	promotional vehicle, re-reg GVS498 by LBL in 1992
1168	London Central - New Cross	
1170	Homegrown, Nairobi, Kenya	re-reg XYJ441 by LBL in 1994, Use unknown
1171	MTL London - Holloway	
1174	London Central - New Cross	
1176	London Central - New Cross	
1180	Routemaster ASBL, Luxembourg	registered B1180, promotional vehicle

1181	Mr P Brandes, Konstanz, Germany	publicity vehicle for the musical 'Cats', bodywork lowered to under 13 foot. registered KN-C-989
1183	London&Country - Leatherhead	
1185	MTL London - Holloway	re-reg XYJ427 in 1994
1187	Nagasaki Ken-ie Bus Co., Nagasaki, Japan	open top + doors fitted, used on sightseeing tours, registered 2454
1192	Mitsubishi Corporation, Japan	location and use unknown
1197	Café de la Croix-Blanche, Posieux, Switzerland	re-reg KGJ29A by LBL in 1990, static coffee shop
1204	London Transport Buses Reserve fleet - Hatfield	in storage
1205	London Transport Buses Reserve fleet - Hatfield	re-reg XYJ429 in1994, in storage
1212	Harbarth & Shenton, Lipperbruch, Germany	
1214	London Transport Buses Reserve fleet - Hatfield	in storage
1218	MTL London	
1221	Mr P Pesikaka, Tottenham, Ontario, Canada	registered HVR203
1224	Bluebird Buses (601) - Perth	re-reg UYJ654 in 1993
1242	Double Deck Tours (8), Niagara, Canada	registered BC8 553, Leyland engine
1243	Negombo Peopolised Transport Services, Negombo Sri Lanka	registered 60 6630
1245	Bluebird Buses (614) - Perth	re-reg LDS210A in 1990
1248	Kariuizawa Classic Car Museum, Nagano, Japan	engine removed prior to export
1251	Unknown owner, Japan	location and use unknown
1257	Homegrown, Nairobi, Kenya	re-reg XYJ442 by LBL in 1994, location and use unknown
1260	London Central - New Cross	
1262	Rural Youth Bus Project, Ely, Cambs.	re-reg VYJ876 in 1993, mobile youth club
1266	Unknown owner, Argentina	location and use unknown
1271	Cabriolet Cars, Funchal, Madeira, Portugal	re-reg RSK254 in 1992, open top 1996
1274	LBPG, Cobham, Surrey	re-reg LDS67A by Stagecoach in 1988, under preparation for sale
1280	Mr J Miller, Enfield	preserved
1282	Pepsi Cola, Istanbul, Turkey	promotional vehicle
1283	MTL London - Holloway	
1287	MTL London - Holloway	withdrawn
1288	Citybus, Kowloon, Hong Kong (1)	rebuilt to vintage open top style and registered HK1931 in 1989, Leyland engine
1289	Bluebird Buses (609) - Perth	re-reg XSL596A in 1990
1292	London Transport Buses Reserve fleet - Hatfield	re-reg NVS485 in 1993, in storage
1294	Negombo Peopolised Transport Services, Negombo, Sri Lanka	registered 60 6637
1305	London Central - New Cross	
1312	Mr M Haynes, Old Coulsdon	preserved, re-reg MFF509 by LBL in 1994, Leyland engine
1313	Unknown owner, USA	location and use unknown
1314	Button Design Contracts, London	location and use unknown
1316	F C Muntaner Mataix, Alicante, Spain	
1321	Mr B Walker, Eastham	preserved
1324	South London - Brixton	Iveco engine fitted in 1993
1330	London Transport Buses Reserve fleet - Hatfield	re-reg KGH975A in 1991, in storage
1336	Sri Lanka Transport Board	registered 60 6608
1339	Yamada Fudousan Co., Osaka, Japan	restaurant
1348	MTL London - Holloway	
1353	Mr J Coombes, Groes Faen, nr. Cardiff	preserved
1357	Blackpool Transport (528)	Leyland engine, in storage
1359	Riparo Auto SNC, Palermo, Sicily, Italy	
1361	South London - Brixton	Iveco engine fitted and re-reg VYJ808 in 1993
1363	Mr C Knight, Badminton	preserved, Leyland engine
1364	Sri Lanka Transport Board	registered 60 6606
1366	Brakell Omnibus Sales (London) Ltd.	re-reg NKH807A by East Yorkshire in 1990

1368	Mr T Murayama, Tokyo, Japan	converted to single-deck by LT in 1975, currently stored in Derbyshire
1371	Abegweit Sightseeing Tours, Charlottetown, Prince Edward Island, Canada	registered PVA046, Leyland engine
1380	London Central - New Cross	
1384	Tea & Pub 'Double Decker', Tokyo, Japan	tea and pub house
1394	Mr H Hobson, Royston, Herts.	Leyland engine
1397	Mr A Naish, Loughborough	preserved, re-reg 71AWN in 1995, Leyland engine
1398	South London - Brixton	Iveco engine fitted and re-reg KGJ118A in 1993
1400	London Central - New Cross	
1401	Sri Lanka Transport Board	registered 60 6639
1403	Mr P & D Sapte et al, Watford	preserved, Leyland engine, open top conversion by LT in 1984
1404	Koyama Driving School, Kanagawa, Japan	Leyland engine, waiting room
1413	Negombo Peopolised Transport Services, Negombo, Sri Lanka	registered 60 6629
1414	Museum of Transport, Manchester	Leyland engine, vehicle donated by LTE
1415	Les Secrets du Musée, Ste Eustache, Quebec, Canada	registered AP.6119, platform doors fitted
1417	Artas Promotions, Budapest, Hungary	Leyland engine
1421	Unknown owner	re-reg AEW440A in 1990
1424	Mr J Klambower, North Gower, Ontario, Canada	out of use, engine removed, last recorded as registered BC9 998
1425	Mr O Fiarce, St Egreve, France	located at Grenoble
1428	London Transport Buses Reserve fleet - Hatfield	in storage
1433	Mr B Maniglia, Minerbio, Italy	Personnel and Motorcycle transporter, roof lowered and partially open top
1448	Drury Lane Dairy Bar, Experimental Farm, Toronto, Ottawa, Canada	registered BC9 997 (but not carried), ice cream parlour, engineless
1449	Mr R Kemp, Battersea	preserved, occasional psv use
1522	Unknown owner, Portoroz, Yugoslavia	condition unknown, Leyland engine
1526	Unknown owner, Spain	Leyland engine
1527	Stagecoach East London - Upton Park	frequently loaned to BBCtv at Elstree for Eastenders TV series
1528	EMS Bus Services, Greasby, Wirral	re-reg KGJ117A by LBL in 1993, Iveco engine fitted 1991, out of use
1530	Sri Lanka Transport Board	registered 60 6607
1531	Unknown owner, Spain	
1539	Unknown owner, Japan	last reported in use as a restaurant, Leyland engine
1543	Mr P Watson, Cheam	preserved, Leyland engine
1545	Exported to Paraguay	location and use unknown, re-reg KGJ37A by LBL in 1991
1546	Unknown owner, Japan	Leyland engine
1548	Double Deck Tours (11), Niagara, Canada	registered BC8 554, Leyland engine
1549	Zakkaya, Saitama, Japan	used as a grocery shop, fitted with platform doors, Leyland engine
1555	Domino Steak House, Eupen, Belgium	re-reg EBY315B by LBL in 1992
1562	London Transport Buses Reserve fleet - Hatfield	in storage
1563	Mr N Townsend, Chiswick	preserved, Leyland engine
1568	MTL London - Holloway	
1571	Routemaster Travel Ltd., Ruislip	Leyland engine, on long term loan to Timebus Travel
1581	Negombo Peopolised Transport Services, Negombo, Sri Lanka	registered 60 6634
1583	Blackpool Transport (521)	Leyland engine, in storage
1585	Unknown owner, France	re-reg ALC459A by LBL in 1994, location and use unknown
1590	Psychiatric Support & Aftercare Workshops, Ashford, Surrey	Iveco engine fitted 1991, door fitted to platform, for use in support of charity
1593	South London - Brixton	Iveco engine fitted in 1991
1599	Bluebird Buses (604) - Perth	re-reg YTS820A in 1987

1604	Beach Bus Co., Kittyhawk, North Carolina, USA	registered ZD3994, open top
1607	Bluebird Buses (607) - Perth	re-reg LDS201A in 1989, currently stored out of use
1609	Exported to France	location and use unknown
1611	The City of Oxford, Oxford, Missouri, USA	open top, used on city sightseeing tours
1618	Double Deck Tours (10), Niagara Falls, Canada	registered BA4 802
1619	Unknown owner, Japan	re-reg KGJ188A by LBL in 1993, location and use unknown
1620	Abegweit Sightseeing Tours, Charlottetown, Prince Edward Island, Canada	registered PVA079, Leyland engine
1621	London Central - New Cross	re-reg KGJ187A in 1993
1627	Blackpool Transport (523)	Leyland engine, in storage
1630	Village Bus (V26), Garston, Merseyside	re-reg EDS537B by Kelvin Scottish in 1988, out of use
1640	Blackpool Transport (524)	Leyland engine, in storage
1641	Blue Triangle, Rainham, Essex	Leyland engine, in storage
1643	Queen Elizabeth Hospital, Edgbaston	Leyland engine, promotional vehicle for the Renal unit
1647	Stagecoach United Counties (706) - Northampton	re-reg BNK32A in 1992, in storage
1649	Sound Prop, Budapest, Hungary	Leyland engine
1650	Blackpool Transport (525)	Leyland engine, in storage
1651	Double Deck Tours (3), Niagara, Canada	registered BA4 805, Leyland engine
1653	Reading Mainline	former promotional vehicle (NILE1), acquired for spares only
1654	Mr D Forrest, Southampton	preserved, Leyland engine
1660	Leisure Concepts Double Decker Bus Tours Division, Queenstown, New Zealand	t/a Arrowtown Sightseeing, Leyland engine, registered NC7416
1666	London Central - New Cross	
1670	Mr M Gibson, Auckland, New Zealand	t/a Double Deck Bus Charters, registered 4HIRE2, Leyland engine
1676	London Transport Buses Reserve fleet - Hatfield	in storage
1677	Bygone Buses, Staplehurst	named Pride of Kent
1681	Unknown owner, France	location and use unknown
1682	McDonalds Restaurants, Germany	children's party bus, location unknown
1684	Last reported as with De Dubbeldekkers, Schilde, Belgium	current location and use unknown, Leyland engine
1691	Mr J Fozard, Shipley	preserved
1694	Ciclo Tours, Santander, Spain	location and use unknown, open top
1699	Messrs S Beere and D Richardson, Sidcup	preserved
1700	MTL London - Holloway	re-reg KGJ167A in 1992
1701	Mr R Hogber, Stockholm, Sweden	registered PAH502
1703	Citybus, Kowloon, Hong Kong (3)	registered EZ8347, open top
1708	Mr & Mrs Collins, Perth, Australia	registered TC2323, used by the Balcotta Primary School at Dianella
1711	Last reported as with De Dubbeldekkers, Schilde, Belgium	current location and use unknown, Leyland engine
1713	Unknown owner, Japan	Leyland engine, in use as a static Café at Mito station
1720	Unknown owner, Portoroz, Yugoslavia	condition unknown, open top, registered KP.109.650, Leyland engine
1725	South London - Brixton	Iveco engine fitted in 1991
1727	Unknown owner	
1730	A C Brain Co., Osaka, Japan	Leyland engine, all over advert livery
1731	Brakell Omnibus Sales (London) Ltd.	
1732	Mr P Roisin, Bus Prophils, Chatelet, Belgium	registered B4383, Leyland engine, rear platform doors fitted
1734	South London - Brixton	Iveco engine fitted in 1991
1735	Blackpool Transport (526)	Leyland engine, in storage
1737	London Transport Museum (donated)	on display at Covent Garden museum
1740	94.7FM Concerto, Montevideo, Uruguay	Leyland engine, platform doors fitted
1741	East Yorkshire (809) - Hull	Leyland engine, re-reg PAG809A in 1994, in storage
1747	London Borough of Wandsworth (1141)	Leyland engine, playbus
1752	Mr T Mulligan, Ontario, Canada	registered BB4 289, engineless, out of use

1754	LA Motor Coach Co., Los Angeles, USA	Leyland engine, open top
1756	Bright Horizon Conservatoire School, Texas, USA	registered U31 275, Leyland engine
1758	MTL London - Holloway	
1767	Wing Fellowship Home, West Bridgeford	promotional vehicle, Leyland engine
1771	Warehouse Night Club, Doncaster	Leyland engine
1773	Piccadilly Bus Tours, Ottawa, Ontario, Canada	registered BB4 292, Leyland engine, open top conversion 1995
1776	Liverline (776) - Bootle	withdrawn
1783	London Coaches - Wandsworth	open top conversion in 1986
1788	Piccadilly Bus Tours, Ottawa, Ontario, Canada	registered BB4 954, Leyland engine
1790	London Borough of Lewisham, London	Leyland engine, door fitted to platform, playbus c/o Poverty Action Group
1791	Mr D Hulst, Lier, Belgium	current use unknown, Leyland engine
1793	Unknown owners, Japan	Leyland engine
1796	Unknown owner, Himegi, Japan	'Game Corner', used as a coin-in-the-slot machine parlour on roof garden of shopping complex, platform doors fitted
1797	London Central - New Cross	
1799	MTL London - Holloway	
1801	South London - Brixton	Iveco engine fitted in 1990
1804	MTL London - Holloway	re-reg EYY327B in 1995
1807	McDonalds Restaurants, Mereside, Lancashire	re-reg EVM132B in 1992, Childrens Party Bus
1810	Martin Dawes Communications, Paris, France	re-reg EBY247B in 1990
1811	South London - Brixton	Iveco engine fitted and re-reg EGF220B in 1990
1815	Hi Klimmet, De Hupberg, Isterberg, Germany	publicity vehicle for Twinings Tea Makers, bodywork lowered to under 13 foot, registered ST EF 65
1819	Glenhills Co., Kagoshima, Japan	Satsuma Eikokukan restaurant
1822	South London - Brixton	Iveco engine fitted in 1990
1825	London Transport Buses Reserve fleet - Hatfield	in storage
1827	Negombo Peopolised Transport Services, Negombo, Sri Lanka	registered 60 6627
1836	Chester Bus & Boat Co., Great Boughton, Chester	re-reg EGF285B by LBL in 1991, open top conversion in 1995
1840	MTL London - Holloway	
1842	Mr I Rushby, Market Rasen	re-reg BFW544B in 1989, mobile home
1843	William Jewel College, Liberty, Missouri, USA	Leyland engine
1851	Sri Lanka Transport Board	registered 60 6601
1859	Reading Mainline (17)	Leyland engine
1864	London Coaches - Wandsworth	open top conversion in 1986, Leyland engine
1871	Mr H Hobson, Royston, Herts.	preserved
1872	South London - Brixton	Iveco engine fitted 1990
1873	Citybus, Kowloon, Hong Kong (2)	rebuilt to vintage open top style and re-reg ES4007 in 1990, Leyland engine
1878	London Borough of Wandsworth (1142)	Leyland engine, playbus
1882	McDonalds Restaurants, Schongau, Germany	children's party bus
1883	Action Car, Koln, Germany	Leyland engine, registered LIP-RM.909
1885	King Food Corporation (Property) Ltd., Potchefstroom, South Africa	registered YBB15167, Leyland engine
1887	Halden Trafikk, Halden, Norway	registered AX32911, Leyland engine
1888	Double Deck Tours (9), Niagara, Canada	registered BA4 850, Leyland engine
1889	Marchen-Japan Co (1)., Tokyo, Japan	Leyland engine, promotional vehicle, offside emergency exits fitted
1897	Staf Cars, Lommel, Belgium	registered GUS594, Leyland engine
1904	Piccadilly Bus Tours, Ottawa, Ontario, Canada	registered BE9 679, Leyland engine
1909	Double Deck Tours (6), Niagara, Canada	registered BA4 804
1911	Anglo European Trade, Budapest, Hungary	re-reg YSL76B by Strathtay Scottish in 1990, current use unknown
1912	Le Grands Pub, Araches, France	converted to a British style pub in the French Alps
1913	Messrs D Bentley & T Worsnop, Halifax	preserved

1916	Queen Victoria Public House, Lloret de Mar, Spain	
1917	Unknown owner, Portoroz, Yugoslavia	condition unknown, Leyland engine
1918	King Food Corporation (Property) Ltd., Potchefstroom, South Africa	Leyland engine
1919	London Coaches - Wandsworth	open top conversion in 1986
1924	McDonalds Restaurants of Canada, Mississauga, Ontario, Canada	registered BE1 823
1930	Cabildo Insular de Lanzarote, Arrecife, Lanzarote	Leyland engine, out of use
1933	Stagecoach Cumberland (904) - Whitehaven	in storage
1936	Blue Triangle, Rainham, Essex	in storage, Leyland engine
1941	Stagecoach Cumberland (902) - Whitehaven	in storage
1943	Piccadilly Bus Tours, Ottawa, Ontario, Canada	registered BB4 951, Leyland engine
1947	Unknown owner, Guststalte Tiechschanke, Geyer, Germany	static restaurant with folding canvas high roof, Leyland engine
1948	Reading Mainline (29)	
1949	Unknown owner, Los Angeles, USA	open top, rebuilt with offside exit, Leyland engine
1950	Piccadilly Bus Tours, Ottawa, Ontario, Canada	registered BB4 953, Leyland engine, open top conversion 1995
1951	94.7FM Concerto, Montevideo, Uruguay	Leyland engine, open top
1955	London Central - New Cross	
1959	Marineland Theme Park, Barcelona, Spain	promotional vehicle
1962	London Central - New Cross	
1966	Blackpool Transport (529)	Leyland engine, in storage
1968	Bluebird Buses (606) - Perth	
1969	Unknown owner, USA	Leyland engine, wine bar at an unknown location
1971	MTL London Northern - Holloway	
1975	Mr D Wright, Paisley	preserved, Leyland engine, named Rory
1977	London Central - New Cross	
1978	South London - Brixton	Iveco engine fitted 1991
1979	MTL London - Holloway	
1980	London Central - New Cross	
1983	Stagecoach Cumberland (903) - Whitehaven	in storage
1986	Sri Lanka Transport Board	registered 60 6618
1988	La Manada Diara Ponet, Lerida, Spain	
1989	Blackpool Transport (530)	Leyland engine, in storage
1990	Reading Mainline (25)	
1991	Antenna Television SA, Maroussi, Athens, Greece	
1993	Mr P Durrant, West Ham	preserved, Leyland engine
2002	City of Collierville, Collierville, Tennessee, USA	re-reg EGF299B by LBL in 1994
2003	Senor I Vargas, Cancun, Mexico	Courtesy bus between The Krytsal Hotel and La Boom Night Club
2005	Dual Way Coaches, Rathcoole, Co. Dublin, Ireland	used to operate Dublin City Tours, registered 64 D 805
2010	Carlton Television Ltd., New Orleans, Lousiana, USA	hospitality unit, Leyland engine
2011	Reading Mainline (4)	Transmatic lighting fitted by Southend Transport in 1988
2017	Chicago Motor Coach Co., (511) Chicago, USA	registered 7936H, open top, rebuilt with offside exit, Leyland engine, out of use
2018	Marchen-Japan Co. (2), Tokyo, Japan	Leyland engine, promotional vehicle, offside emergency exits fitted
2021	London Transport Buses Reserve fleet - Hatfield	in storage
2022	London Central - New Cross	
2023	MTL London - Holloway	
2024	Stagecoach Cumberland (901) - Whitehaven	in storage
2026	Koyama Driving School, Kanagawa, Japan	waiting room, Leyland engine
2032	Societé des Autocars Brouens, Villeneuve sur Lot, France	registered 4123-RW-47
2033	London Transport Buses Reserve fleet - Hatfield	in storage
2034	Reading Mainline(1)	Transmatic lighting fitted by Southend Transport in 1988
2037	Mr E Rayner, Bracknell	preserved, Leyland engine
2041	MTL London - Holloway	
2043	Koyama Driving School, Kanagawa, Japan	waiting room, Leyland engine

Number	Owner / Location	Notes
2046	Unknown owner, Argentina	location and use unknown
2049	Sri Lanka Transport Board	registered 60 6617
2050	London Transport Buses Reserve fleet - Hatfield	in storage
2051	London Central - New Cross	
2059	Mr A Haywood, Bromley	Leyland engine occasionally loaned to Delaine (113)
2060	Stagecoach Ribble - Blackburn	in storage
2063	Mr S Levy, Harare, Zimbabwe	registered 531 647B, used to transport old age pensioners to a restaurant in Borrowdale village
2065	East Yorkshire (812) - Hull	in storage under conversion to open top
2071	Blackpool Transport (531)	Leyland engine, in storage
2077	Unknown owner, Argentina	location and use unknown
2078	London Transport Buses Reserve fleet - Hatfield	in storage
2081	Blue Triangle, Rainham, Essex	re-reg EDS620B by Kelvin Central Buses in1993, in storage
2083	Bournemouth Passenger Transport Association - Hurn	Clydemaster refurbishment in 1987, not operated in passenger service with this owner, in storage
2087	Anglo European Trade, Budapest, Hungary	current use unknown
2088	Negombo Peopolised Transport Services, Negombo Sri Lanka	registered 60 6638
2089	Blackpool Transport (533)	Leyland engine, in storage
2092	Sri Lanka Transport Board	registered 60 6616
2097	London Transport Buses Reserve fleet - Hatfield	in storage
2100	K K B Tarsasag, Szent, Istvan, Hungary	
2101	McDonalds Restaurants, Apolda, near Weimar, Germany	children's party bus
2103	Freight Media, London	promotional vehicle
2106	London Central - New Cross	
2107	Mr R Dale, Streatham	preserved, Leyland engine
2109	London Central - New Cross	
2113	Marchen-Japan Co., Tokyo, Japan	promotional vehicle
2114	Anglo European Trade, Budapest, Hungary	current use unknown
2116	Messrs G Lunn & T Muir, Egham	preserved in '1933' livery
2120	last reported with Teleticke Gmbh, Hamburg, Germany	registered HH-ED 930, fitted with lightweight lifting roof, current location and use unknown
2121	Mr B Turner, Bridge of Weir	preserved
2122	Stagecoach Ribble - Blackburn	in storage
2124	Brakell Omnibus Sales (London) Ltd.	under preparation for sale
2128	London Central - New Cross	
2129	Armitage, Barnsley	
2131	Fukunishi Company Ltd., Osaka, Japan	location and use unknown
2133	Royal Blue Line Motor Tours, Victoria, British Columbia, Canada	
2136	MTL London - Holloway	
2145	Coffee & Beer London Bus, Saitama, Japan	coffee and beer house
2150	Unknown owner, Tokyo, Japan	use unknown
2151	London Central - New Cross	
2152	Mr M Overcash, Atlanta, USA	t/a Great Knight Tours
2153	MTL London - Holloway	
2154	Mr J Gowdy, Ballyclare, Northern Ireland	preserved
2155	Sri Lanka Transport Board	registered 60 6605, Ashok engine
2156	Timebus Travel, St Albans	H36/24R
2158	Sri Lanka Transport Board (KS79) - Kandy	registered 60 6615
2160	Sri Lanka Transport Board	registered 60 6614
2162	Double Deck Tours (14), Niagara Canada	registered BA4 813
2165	Double Deck Tours (4), Niagara Canada	registered BA4 814
2166	Sakurai Ham, Kanagawa, Japan	party bus
2171	Royal Oman Police, Oman	
2173	London Transport Buses Reserve fleet - Hatfield	in storage
2174	Mr P Pesikaka, Tottenham, Ontario, Canada	registered HVR007
2178	Pan Britannica Industries Ltd., Waltham Abbey	promotional vehicle, 'The Bio Garden Bus'

2179	South London - Brixton	Iveco engine fitted in 1990
2180	Timebus Travel, St. Albans	H36/24R
2181	Unknown owner, California, USA	open top
2183	Messrs A Rahman & Taher, Dubai, United Arab Emirates	registered 23428
2185	South London - Brixton	Iveco engine fitted 1993
2186	MTL London - Holloway	
2187	Homegrown, Nairobi, Kenya	location and use unknown
2192	Stagecoach United Counties (708) - Northampton	in storage
2193	Marchen-Japan Co., Tokyo, Japan	promotional vehicle
2198	Mr M Drabwell, Bushey	preserved, on long term loan to Timebus Travel
2200	Octobus SARL, Paris, France	
2201	Reading Mainline (21)	under preparation for service
2203	Messrs Nelson & Kennedy, Penicuik, Edinburgh	
2205	S Hori & Partners, Budapest, Hungary	
2206	Double Deck Tours (7), Niagara, Canada	registered BA4 803, Leyland engine
2207	Sri Lanka Transport Board	registered 60 6602
2208	Mr M King, Leeds	preserved in Shillibeer livery
2209	Beach Bus Co., Kittyhawk, North Carolina, USA	
2210	East Yorkshire (816) - Hull	in storage
2212	Mr H Schulsves, Rosengarten-Ehestorf, Germany	rebuilt open top with staircase on the nearside, registered HH-MM-278
2213	London Transport Buses Reserve fleet - Hatfield	in storage
2217	South London - Brixton	Iveco engine fitted in 1991

RMC

4	London&Country - Reigate	Leyland engine, semi preserved
1453	Leaside Buses - Tottenham	under preparation for service
1456	Stagecoach East London - Upton Park	re-reg LFF875 in 1994
1458	Unknown owner, Quimper, France	registered 115-WX-29
1459	Mr P Almeroth, Romford	preserved
1461	Stagecoach East London - Upton Park	Green Line livery
1462	Nostalgiabus, Mitcham	
1464	Leaside Buses - Tottenham	open top conversion in 1990, Iveco engine fitted in 1992, named Princess
1469	London United - Fulwell	recruitment vehicle, out of use
1474	Mr G Laming, Coulsdon	
1476	Mr E Knorn, Swindon	preserved
1477	Blue Triangle, Rainham, Essex	in storage
1480	Mr Jan-Ake Haggren, Vastra Froluna, Sweden	registered PBA541, promotional vehicle for Coca-Cola
1481	Mr B Venhofen, Bremerhaven, Germany	open top
1485	Stagecoach East London - Upton Park	
1486	Unknown owner, Germany	re-reg KVS276 by LBL in 1992
1487	Mr D Sullivan, Harrow	preserved
1488	Aids Awareness Campaign, Paris, France	promotional vehicle
1490	Bluebird Buses (608) - Perth	in storage
1492	CentreWest - Training fleet	recruitment vehicle, named Ruby, out of use
1495	Miss B Sears, Addlestone	mobile catering vehicle, t/a Bus Stop Catering, named Gus
1496	Sextons Hi-fi, Fulham, London	
1497	Mr R C Gale, Avonwick	preserved
1499	Mr P Kane, Perpignon, France	promotional vehicle
1500	Mr P Hodgson, Romford	preserved, re-reg ALC368A by LBL in 1991
1503	Herve SARL, Vannes, France	registered 7806-TL-56, promotional vehicle
1507	Mr R Humphries, Dagenham	preserved

1510	CentreWest - Westbourne Park	open top conversion in 1989, Cummins engine fitted and Transmatic lighting fitted to the lower deck in 1993
1513	Metroline - Cricklewood	
1515	Stagecoach Selkent - in storage at Whitehaven	open top conversion in 1987
1516	Mr P Almeroth, Romford	preserved
1519	Mr J-L Sastre, Marseille, France	Piazza restaurant,
		registered 6005-RR-13

RCL

2218	London Borough of Redbridge - Goodmayes	mobile family day centre
2219	BaMMOT, Wythall	preserved
2220	London Coaches - Wandsworth	convertible open top 1991
2221	LRT Central Distribution Services, Acton	exhibition vehicle, available for hire
2223	AVS Graphics Ltd., Farnham	hospitality vehicle
2226	Luna Film Transport, Chertsey	catering vehicle
2229	London Transport Museum (donated)	undergoing restoration
2233	Mr A Brown, Romford	preserved
2235	London Coaches - Wandsworth	convertible open top 1990
2238	Abada Film Services, Weybridge	catering vehicle
2239	Blue Triangle, Rainham, Essex	
2240	London Coaches - Wandsworth	convertible open top 1991
2241	London Coaches - Wandsworth	convertible open top 1991
2243	London Coaches - Wandsworth	convertible open top 1990
2245	London Coaches - Wandsworth	convertible open top 1991
2248	London Coaches - Wandsworth	convertible open top 1991
2250	London Coaches - Wandsworth	convertible open top 1991
2252	Double Deck Tours (2), Niagara, Canada	registered BC8 559
2253	London Coaches - Wandsworth	convertible open top 1991
2254	Mrs J V Hart, Harrow	preserved
2255	Double Deck Tours (1), Niagara, Canada	registered BC8 555
2256	Brakell Omnibus Sales (London) Ltd.	
2259	London Coaches - Wandsworth	convertible open top 1991
2260	London Coaches - Wandsworth	

RMF/former Northern General vehicles
[All are Leyland engined unless detailed]

RMF1254	Mr M Biddell, Woodford	preserved
RCN689	Page Motors, Poole	promotional vehicle
RCN699	Go-Ahead Northern Bus Enthusiasts Association	preserved, re-reg PCN762 in 1996, AEC engine, occasional psv use
RCN701	Time Travel, Thornton Heath	numbered RMF2771
EUP405B	Mr D Slater, Newcastle	preserved
FPT580C	Creamobil, Schoten, Belgium	open top, AEC engine
FPT581C	New Cross Playbus Association, London	playbus, for sale
FPT588C	The Big Bus Co., London (RMF588)	open top
FPT589C	Palladium Disco, Coslada, near Madrid, Spain	static advert for discothèque
FPT590C	Mr G Matthews, Sidcup	preserved, AEC engine
FPT591C	London Bus Transport, Espoo, Finland	
FPT592C	The Big Bus Co., London (RMF592)	AEC engine
FPT603C	The Big Bus Co., London	under preparation for service, numbered RMF2809 when preserved

FRM

1   London Transport Museum (donated)   occasional psv use

RMA/former BEA vehicles
[Vehicles are listed in RMA number order with the former BEA number shown in brackets.]

1	(21)	Mr A Henderson, Cambridge	preserved
5	(35)	Stagecoach East London - Upton Park	named King Charles II in 1991
6	(38)	Mr R Higgins, Reading	preserved
8	(40)	Stagecoach East London - Upton Park	
9	(46)	Mr A Boath, Norwood Green	
10	(47)	Mr R Brown, Motcombe	in storage
11	(48)	Green Rover, Watford	withdrawn, in storage
13	(56)	Mr J M Roberts, Kentish Town	preserved
14	(2)	Green Rover, Watford	withdrawn, in storage
15	(11)	Blue Triangle, Rainham, Essex	in storage
16	(14)	London&Country - Leatherhead	Clydemaster refurbishment and named 'George the Routemaster' by Clydeside Scottish in 1989, under preparation for service
17	(17)	Octobus SARL, Paris, France	
19	(22)	Mr D Horder, Daventry	Luxury mobile caravan
20	(33)	London Street, Romagne, Lavoux, France	registered 1457-SQ-86, promotional vehicle
22	(45)	J J Kavanagh & Sons Ltd., Urlingford, Co. Kilkenny, Ireland	registered 67 KK 501
23	(49)	Unknown owner, West Midlands	former promotional vehicle, two staircases at rear, current location and use unknown
25	(53)	Dual Way Coaches, Rathcoole, Co. Dublin, Ireland	used to operate Dublin City Tours, registered 67-D-813, open top conversion in 1995
26	(60)	Dual Way Coaches, Rathcoole, Co. Dublin, Ireland	used to operate Dublin City Tours, registered 67-D-816
28	(1)	Mr J Stoute, Witton	preserved
29	(3)	Mr R Brown, Motcombe	currently being rebuilt
37	(12)	Mr R Brown, Motcombe	used by Shaftesbury & District
47	(30)	Mr R Higgins, Reading	preserved, former trainer (ie staircase removed)
48	(31)	Blue Triangle, Rainham, Essex	in storage
49	(32)	Blue Triangle, Rainham, Essex (RMS49)	mainly used on sightseeing duties
50	(34)	Bluebird Buses (651) - Perth	in storage
51	(36)	Blue Triangle, Rainham, Essex	in storage
52	(37)	Time Travel, Thornton Heath	
53	(41)	Mr A Boath, Norwood Green	promotional/hospitality vehicle
55	(44)	London United - Fulwell	trainer (ie staircase removed), out of use
56	(51)	Octobus SARL, Paris, France	registered 401-KPT-75
57	(54)	Mr M Alder, Clacton-on-Sea	used by Time Travel
58	(55)	Mr D Forest, Bootle, Merseyside	on long term loan to MTL, out of use
62	(62)	London Borough of Ealing - Greenford	playbus
65	(65)	Mr J Letts, Gillingham, Dorset	occasional psv use, t/a Red Bus

RML

No.	Operator	Notes
880	London United - Shepherds Bush	Cummins engine fitted in 1993, London United livery & numbered ER880 in 1989, refurbished in 1993
881	London United - Shepherds Bush	Cummins engine fitted in 1992, refurbished in 1993
882	Leaside Buses - Clapton	Cummins engine fitted in 1991, refurbished in 1992
883	London Central - Camberwell	Cummins engine fitted in 1991, refurbished in 1992
884	Leaside Buses - Clapton	Cummins engine fitted in 1990, refurbished in 1992
885	CentreWest - Westbourne Park	Cummins engine fitted in 1990, refurbished in 1992
886	Stagecoach East London - Upton Park	Cummins engine fitted in 1990, refurbished in 1992
887	London General - Putney	Iveco engine fitted in 1990, refurbished in 1993
888	Leaside Buses - Clapton	Cummins engine fitted in 1990, refurbished in 1992
889	London General - Putney	Iveco engine fitted in 1991, refurbished in 1993
890	Stagecoach East London - Upton Park	Cummins engine fitted in 1991, refurbished in 1992, re-reg XFF814 in 1995
891	London United - Shepherds Bush	Cummins engine fitted in 1991, refurbished in 1993
892	South London - Brixton	Iveco engine fitted in 1991, refurbished in 1992
893	Metroline - Willesden	Cummins engine fitted in 1990, refurbished in 1993, re-reg KFF276 in 1994
894	London General - Waterloo	Iveco engine fitted in 1991, refurbished in 1992
895	South London - Brixton	Iveco engine fitted in 1991, refurbished in 1992
896	Leaside Buses - Clapton	Cummins engine fitted in 1992, refurbished in 1993
897	Leaside Buses - Clapton	Cummins engine fitted in 1993, refurbished in 1993
898	Stagecoach East London - Bow	Iveco engine fitted in 1993, refurbished in 1993, re-reg XFF813 in 1995
899	London General - Putney	Iveco engine fitted in 1992, refurbished in 1992
900	Blue Triangle, Rainham, Essex	Clydemaster refurbishment by Clydeside in 1988, in storage
901	Leaside Buses - Clapton	Cummins engine fitted in 1990, refurbished in 1992
902	Metroline - Willesden	Cummins engine fitted in 1993, refurbished in 1993, re-reg ALC464A in 1994
903	MTL London - Holloway	Cummins engine fitted in 1990, refurbished in 1992
2261	Leaside Buses - Tottenham	Iveco engine fitted in 1991, refurbished in 1992
2262	London General - Waterloo	Iveco engine fitted in 1991, refurbished in 1992
2263	London General - Waterloo	Iveco engine fitted in 1991, refurbished in 1992
2264	South London - Brixton	Cummins engine fitted in 1992, refurbished in 1993
2265	BTS Coaches - Borehamwood	Iveco engine fitted in 1990, refurbished in 1993
2266	Kentish Bus- Battersea	Cummins engine fitted in 1990, refurbished in 1992
2267	Leaside Buses - Tottenham	Cummins engine fitted in 1991, refurbished in 1994
2268	CentreWest - Westbourne Park	Cummins engine fitted in 1990, refurbished in 1992
2269	London United - Shepherds Bush	Cummins engine fitted in 1991, refurbished in 1993
2270	London Central - Camberwell	Cummins engine fitted in 1991, refurbished in 1993
2271	London Central - New Cross	Cummins engine fitted in 1993, refurbished in 1993
2272	Stagecoach East London - Upton Park	Cummins engine fitted in 1991, refurbished in 1994
2273	London Central - Camberwell	Cummins engine fitted in 1992, refurbished in 1994
2274	Metroline - Willesden	Cummins engine fitted in 1991, refurbished in 1992
2275	London Central - Camberwell	Cummins engine fitted in 1991, refurbished in 1992
2276	London Central - Camberwell	Cummins engine fitted in 1991, refurbished in 1993
2277	Leaside Buses - Tottenham	Cummins engine fitted in 1991, refurbished in 1993
2278	CentreWest - Westbourne Park	Cummins engine fitted in 1991, refurbished in 1994
2279	London Central - Camberwell	Cummins engine fitted in 1992, refurbished in 1993
2280	Leaside Buses - Clapton	Cummins engine fitted in 1992, refurbished in 1994
2281	CentreWest - Westbourne Park	Cummins engine fitted in 1991, refurbished in 1992
2282	MTL London - Holloway	Cummins engine fitted in 1992, refurbished in 1993
2283	London Central - New Cross	Cummins engine fitted in 1992, refurbished in 1993
2284	MTL London - Holloway	Cummins engine fitted in 1993, refurbished in 1993
2285	Metroline - Willesden	Cummins engine fitted in 1991, refurbished in 1992
2286	Stagecoach East London - Upton Park	Cummins engine fitted in 1991, refurbished in 1992
2287	Leaside Buses - Clapton	Cummins engine fitted in 1993, refurbished in 1993
2288	Metroline - Willesden	Cummins engine fitted in 1993, refurbished in 1993
2289	Metroline - Willesden	Iveco engine fitted in 1991, refurbished in 1993
2290	London General - Putney	Cummins engine fitted in 1991, refurbished in 1992
2291	CentreWest - Westbourne Park	

2292	Leaside Buses - Tottenham	Cummins engine fitted in 1991, refurbished in 1992
2293	London United - Shepherds Bush	Cummins engine fitted in 1992, refurbished in 1993
2294	Leaside Buses - Tottenham	Cummins engine fitted in 1990, refurbished in 1992
2295	MTL London - Holloway	Cummins engine fitted in 1992, refurbished in 1993
2296	MTL London - Holloway	Cummins engine fitted in 1991, refurbished in 1992
2297	London General - Putney	Iveco engine fitted in 1991, refurbished in 1992
2298	London United - Shepherds Bush	Cummins engine fitted in 1991, refurbished in 1992
2299	Metroline - Willesden	Cummins engine fitted in 1993, refurbished in 1994
2300	Stagecoach East London - Bow	Iveco engine fitted in 1992, refurbished in 1993
2301	Kentish Bus- Battersea	Iveco engine fitted in 1990, refurbished in 1993
2302	London Central - Camberwell	Cummins engine fitted in 1991, refurbished in 1994
2303	Stagecoach East London - Bow	Iveco engine fitted in 1992, refurbished in 1993
2304	Leaside Buses - Clapton	Cummins engine fitted in 1991, refurbished in 1993
2305	London General - Waterloo	Iveco engine fitted in 1991, refurbished in 1993
2307	South London - Brixton	Iveco engine fitted in 1992, refurbished in 1993
2308	Metroline - Willesden	Cummins engine fitted in 1993, refurbished in 1994
2309	CentreWest - Westbourne Park	Cummins engine fitted in 1991, refurbished in 1993
2310	MTL London - Holloway	Cummins engine fitted in 1992, refurbished in 1993
2311	Stagecoach East London - Upton Park	Cummins engine fitted in 1991, refurbished in 1992
2312	Metroline - Willesden	Cummins engine fitted in 1993, refurbished in 1994
2313	CentreWest - Westbourne Park	Cummins engine fitted in 1991, refurbished in 1994
2314	London Central - Camberwell	Cummins engine fitted in 1992, refurbished in 1993
2315	Leaside Buses - Tottenham	Cummins engine fitted in 1990, refurbished in 1993
2316	London General - Putney	Iveco engine fitted in 1991, refurbished in 1992
2317	London General - Waterloo	Iveco engine fitted in 1991, refurbished in 1993
2318	London Central - New Cross	Cummins engine fitted in 1991, refurbished in 1993
2321	London General - Putney	Iveco engine fitted in 1992, refurbished in 1993
2322	BTS Coaches - Borehamwood	Cummins engine fitted in 1991, refurbished in 1993
2323	Leaside Buses - Tottenham	Cummins engine fitted in 1991, refurbished in 1993
2324	South London - Brixton	Iveco engine fitted in 1991, refurbished in 1993
2325	Leaside Buses - Clapton	Cummins engine fitted in 1990, refurbished in 1992
2326	Leaside Buses - Clapton	Cummins engine fitted in 1990, refurbished in 1992
2327	London Central - Camberwell	Cummins engine fitted in 1992, refurbished in 1993
2328	Leaside Buses - Clapton	Cummins engine fitted in 1990, refurbished in 1992
2329	Leaside Buses - Clapton	Cummins engine fitted in 1990, refurbished in 1992
2330	Leaside Buses - Tottenham	Cummins engine fitted in 1990, refurbished in 1993
2331	Metroline - Willesden	Cummins engine fitted in 1992, refurbished in 1993
2332	London Central - New Cross	Cummins engine fitted in 1990, refurbished in 1992
2333	South London - Brixton	Iveco engine fitted in 1992, refurbished in 1993
2334	Leaside Buses - Clapton	Cummins engine fitted in 1990, refurbished in 1993
2335	London Central - Camberwell	Cummins engine fitted in 1990, refurbished in 1994
2336	London Central - Camberwell	Cummins engine fitted in 1990, refurbished in 1992
2338	London Central - Camberwell	Cummins engine fitted in 1991, refurbished in 1993
2339	London Central - New Cross	Cummins engine fitted in 1991, refurbished in 1993
2340	Leaside Buses - Tottenham	Cummins engine fitted in 1991, refurbished in 1993
2341	BTS Coaches - Borehamwood	Cummins engine fitted in 1992, refurbished in 1993
2342	London General - Waterloo	Iveco engine fitted in 1991, refurbished in 1992
2343	Kentish Bus - Battersea	Iveco engine fitted in 1991, refurbished in 1993
2344	Leaside Buses - Clapton	Cummins engine fitted in 1991, refurbished in 1992
2345	London Central - New Cross	Cummins engine fitted in 1991, refurbished in 1993
2346	Leaside Buses - Tottenham	Cummins engine fitted in 1991, refurbished in 1992
2347	Kentish Bus - Battersea	Iveco engine fitted in 1991, refurbished in 1993
2348	Metroline - Willesden	Cummins engine fitted in 1993, refurbished in 1994
2349	London United - Shepherds Bush	Cummins engine fitted in 1992, refurbished in 1993
2350	Leaside Buses - Tottenham	Cummins engine fitted in 1991, refurbished in 1993
2351	South London - Brixton	Iveco engine fitted in 1992, refurbished in 1994
2352	CentreWest - Westbourne Park	Cummins engine fitted in 1991, refurbished in 1992
2353	London United - Shepherds Bush	Cummins engine fitted in 1991, refurbished in 1992
2354	Leaside Buses - Clapton	Cummins engine fitted in 1990, refurbished in 1992
2355	Leaside Buses - Clapton	Cummins engine fitted in 1990, refurbished in 1992
2356	Leaside Buses - Clapton	Cummins engine fitted in 1990, refurbished in 1992
2357	CentreWest - Westbourne Park	Cummins engine fitted in 1992, refurbished in 1993
2358	London General - Waterloo	Iveco engine fitted in 1991, refurbished in 1992
2359	Leaside Buses - Clapton	Cummins engine fitted in 1991, refurbished in 1993

2360	London General - Waterloo	Iveco engine fitted in 1990, refurbished in 1992
2361	London General - Putney	Iveco engine fitted in 1991, refurbished in 1992
2362	London Central - Camberwell	Cummins engine fitted in 1990, refurbished in 1994
2363	London General - Waterloo	Iveco engine fitted in 1992, refurbished in 1992
2364	London General - Putney	Iveco engine fitted in 1990, refurbished in 1993
2365	CentreWest - Westbourne Park	Cummins engine fitted in 1991, refurbished in 1993
2366	South London - Brixton	Iveco engine fitted in 1991, refurbished in 1992
2367	MTL London - Holloway	Cummins engine fitted in 1992, refurbished in 1992
2368	Metroline - Willesden	Cummins engine fitted in 1992, refurbished in 1993
2369	CentreWest - Westbourne Park	Cummins engine fitted in 1990, refurbished in 1994
2370	Leaside Buses - Clapton	Cummins engine fitted in 1990, refurbished in 1992
2371	London General - Putney	Iveco engine fitted in 1991, refurbished in 1992
2372	Leaside Buses - Tottenham	Cummins engine fitted in 1990, refurbished in 1993
2373	Leaside Buses - Tottenham	Cummins engine fitted in 1990, refurbished in 1992
2374	CentreWest - Westbourne Park	Cummins engine fitted in 1992, refurbished in 1992
2375	South London - Brixton	Iveco engine fitted in 1991, refurbished in 1993
2376	London General - Putney	Iveco engine fitted in 1990, refurbished in 1993
2377	Metroline - Willesden	Cummins engine fitted in 1993, refurbished in 1994
2378	CentreWest - Westbourne Park	Cummins engine fitted in 1991, refurbished in 1993
2379	CentreWest - Westbourne Park	Cummins engine fitted in 1990, refurbished in 1993
2380	Leaside Buses - Tottenham	Cummins engine fitted in 1990, refurbished in 1992
2381	London Central - Camberwell	Cummins engine fitted in 1990, refurbished in 1993
2382	Kentish Bus - Battersea	Iveco engine fitted in 1991, refurbished in 1993
2383	Kentish Bus - Battersea	Iveco engine fitted in 1991, refurbished in 1993
2384	Metroline - Willesden	Cummins engine fitted in 1992, refurbished in 1993
2385	London General - Waterloo	Iveco engine fitted in 1991, refurbished in 1992
2386	Leaside Buses - Clapton	Cummins engine fitted in 1991, refurbished in 1992
2387	Kentish Bus - Battersea	Iveco engine fitted in 1990, refurbished in 1993
2388	CentreWest - Westbourne Park	Cummins engine fitted in 1990, refurbished in 1993
2389	London General - Waterloo	Iveco engine fitted in 1991, refurbished in 1993
2390	CentreWest - Westbourne Park	Cummins engine fitted in 1990, refurbished in 1994
2391	Leaside Buses - Tottenham	Cummins engine fitted in 1991, refurbished in 1993
2392	Stagecoach East London - Bow	Iveco engine fitted in 1992, refurbished in 1993
2393	MTL London - Holloway	Cummins engine fitted in 1992, refurbished in 1993
2394	Leaside Buses - Tottenham	Cummins engine fitted in 1990, refurbished in 1993
2395	MTL London - Holloway	Cummins engine fitted in 1991, refurbished in 1992
2396	London Central - Camberwell	Cummins engine fitted in 1990, refurbished in 1992
2397	London Central - Camberwell	Cummins engine fitted in 1992, refurbished in 1993
2398	London General - Putney	Iveco engine fitted in 1991, refurbished in 1992
2399	Stagecoach East London - Bow	Iveco engine fitted in 1992, refurbished in 1993
2400	London Central - Camberwell	Cummins engine fitted in 1991, refurbished in 1993
2401	Leaside Buses - Clapton	Cummins engine fitted in 1991, refurbished in 1993
2402	Stagecoach East London - Bow	Iveco engine fitted in 1992, refurbished in 1992
2403	London General - Waterloo	Iveco engine fitted in 1991, refurbished in 1993
2404	BTS Coaches - Borehamwood	Cummins engine fitted in 1993, refurbished in 1993
2405	CentreWest - Westbourne Park	Cummins engine fitted in 1991, refurbished in 1993
2406	Leaside Buses - Clapton	Cummins engine fitted in 1990, refurbished in 1992
2407	South London - Brixton	Iveco engine fitted in 1991, refurbished in 1992
2408	Leaside Buses - Tottenham	Cummins engine fitted in 1990, refurbished in 1994
2409	Leaside Buses - Clapton	Cummins engine fitted in 1992, refurbished in 1993
2410	Kentish Bus- Battersea	Iveco engine fitted in 1991, refurbished in 1993
2411	London Central - Camberwell	Cummins engine fitted in 1990, refurbished in 1993
2412	London General - Putney	Iveco engine fitted in 1992, refurbished in 1992
2413	MTL London - Holloway	Cummins engine fitted in 1992, refurbished in 1992
2414	London United - Shepherds Bush	Cummins engine fitted in 1990, refurbished in 1992
2415	Stagecoach East London - Bow	Iveco engine fitted in 1992, refurbished in 1992
2416	Leaside Buses - Clapton	Cummins engine fitted in 1991, refurbished in 1992
2418	Leaside Buses - Tottenham	Cummins engine fitted in 1990, refurbished in 1992
2419	MTL London - Holloway	Cummins engine fitted in 1992, refurbished in 1993
2422	London General - Putney	Iveco engine fitted in 1991, refurbished in 1992
2428	CentreWest - Westbourne Park	Cummins engine fitted in 1990, refurbished in 1993
2429	Stagecoach East London - Bow	Iveco engine fitted in 1992, refurbished in 1992
2430	Metroline - Willesden	Cummins engine fitted in 1993, refurbished in 1993
2431	Metroline - Willesden	Cummins engine fitted in 1992, refurbished in 1993

2432	London United - Shepherds Bush	Cummins engine fitted in 1990, refurbished in 1992
2434	Leaside Buses - Tottenham	Cummins engine fitted in 1991, refurbished in 1992
2435	Stagecoach East London - Bow	Iveco engine fitted in 1992, refurbished in 1993
2437	Stagecoach East London - Bow	Iveco engine fitted in 1992, refurbished in 1993
2439	Metroline - Willesden	Cummins engine fitted in 1993, refurbished in 1993
2440	London Central - Camberwell	Cummins engine fitted in 1991, refurbished in 1993
2441	London General - Putney	Iveco engine fitted in 1990, refurbished in 1993
2442	CentreWest - Westbourne Park	Cummins engine fitted in 1990, refurbished in 1992
2443	BTS Coaches - Borehamwood	Cummins engine fitted in 1993, refurbished in 1993
2444	Stagecoach East London - Bow	Iveco engine fitted in 1992, refurbished in 1993
2445	Stagecoach East London - Upton Park	Cummins engine fitted in 1991, refurbished in 1992
2446	Metroline - Willesden	Cummins engine fitted in 1992, refurbished in 1993
2447	London United - Shepherds Bush	Cummins engine fitted in 1990, refurbished in 1992
2450	Stagecoach East London - Bow	Iveco engine fitted in 1992, refurbished in 1993
2451	Stagecoach East London - Bow	Iveco engine fitted in 1992, refurbished in 1993
2452	Kentish Bus- Battersea	Iveco engine fitted in 1991, refurbished in 1993
2453	London General - Putney	Iveco engine fitted in 1990, refurbished in 1992
2454	London Central - Camberwell	Cummins engine fitted in 1991, refurbished in 1993
2455	London United - Shepherds Bush	Cummins engine fitted in 1993, refurbished in 1993
2456	Stagecoach East London - Upton Park	Cummins engine fitted in 1990, refurbished in 1992
2457	Leaside Buses - Clapton	Cummins engine fitted in 1990, refurbished in 1992
2460	Leaside Buses - Tottenham	Cummins engine fitted in 1990, refurbished in 1992
2461	London General - Putney	Iveco engine fitted in 1990, refurbished in 1992
2462	Stagecoach East London - Bow	Iveco engine fitted in 1992, refurbished in 1993
2463	London United - Shepherds Bush	Cummins engine fitted in 1992, refurbished in 1992
2464	London United - Shepherds Bush	Cummins engine fitted in 1991, refurbished in 1992
2465	London General - Waterloo	Iveco engine fitted in 1991, refurbished in 1992
2466	London General - Putney	Iveco engine fitted in 1990, refurbished in 1993
2467	CentreWest - Westbourne Park	Cummins engine fitted in 1991, refurbished in 1993
2468	Leaside Buses - Tottenham	Cummins engine fitted in 1991, refurbished in 1993
2469	London Central - Camberwell	Cummins engine fitted in 1991, refurbished in 1994
2470	Stagecoach East London - Bow	Iveco engine fitted in 1992, refurbished in 1993
2471	Metroline - Willesden	Cummins engine fitted in 1992, refurbished in 1993
2472	London General - Putney	Iveco engine fitted in 1990, refurbished in 1993
2473	CentreWest - Westbourne Park	Cummins engine fitted in 1992, refurbished in 1993
2474	London Central - Camberwell	Cummins engine fitted in 1991, refurbished in 1994
2475	London General - Putney	Iveco engine fitted in 1991, refurbished in 1992
2476	CentreWest - Westbourne Park	Cummins engine fitted in 1990, refurbished in 1994
2477	South London - Brixton	Iveco engine fitted in 1991, refurbished in 1992
2478	Metroline - Willesden	Cummins engine fitted in 1991, refurbished in 1993
2479	MTL London - Holloway	Cummins engine fitted in 1993, refurbished in 1993
2480	CentreWest - Westbourne Park	Cummins engine fitted in 1991, refurbished in 1993
2481	Stagecoach East London - Bow	Iveco engine fitted in 1992, refurbished in 1993
2482	London Central - Camberwell	Cummins engine fitted in 1990, refurbished in 1994
2483	Leaside Buses - Clapton	Cummins engine fitted in 1991, refurbished in 1992
2484	London Central - Camberwell	Cummins engine fitted in 1990, refurbished in 1994
2485	London United - Shepherds Bush	Cummins engine fitted in 1993, refurbished in 1993
2486	CentreWest - Westbourne Park	Cummins engine fitted in 1990, refurbished in 1993
2487	BTS Coaches - Borehamwood	Cummins engine fitted in 1990, refurbished in 1993
2488	Stagecoach East London - Bow	Iveco engine fitted in 1992, refurbished in 1992
2489	London United - Shepherds Bush	Cummins engine fitted in 1992, refurbished in 1992
2490	CentreWest - Westbourne Park	Cummins engine fitted in 1992, refurbished in 1993
2491	South London - Brixton	Iveco engine fitted in 1991, refurbished in 1993
2492	Leaside Buses - Clapton	Cummins engine fitted in 1991, refurbished in 1992
2493	Stagecoach East London - Bow	Iveco engine fitted in 1992, refurbished in 1993
2494	Leaside Buses - Clapton	Cummins engine fitted in 1992, refurbished in 1993
2495	Stagecoach East London - Upton Park	Cummins engine fitted in 1990, refurbished in 1993
2496	Stagecoach East London - Upton Park	Cummins engine fitted in 1991, refurbished in 1992
2497	Stagecoach East London - Upton Park	Cummins engine fitted in 1991, refurbished in 1992
2498	CentreWest - Westbourne Park	Cummins engine fitted in 1990, refurbished in 1992
2499	London Central - Camberwell	Cummins engine fitted in 1991, refurbished in 1994
2500	London United - Shepherds Bush	Cummins engine fitted in 1990, refurbished in 1992
2501	CentreWest - Westbourne Park	Cummins engine fitted in 1991, refurbished in 1994
2502	London General - Putney	Iveco engine fitted in 1991, refurbished in 1993

2503	Leaside Buses - Tottenham	Cummins engine fitted in 1991, refurbished in 1993
2504	Leaside Buses - Tottenham	Cummins engine fitted in 1990, refurbished in 1993
2505	Kentish Bus- Battersea	Iveco engine fitted in 1990, refurbished in 1993
2506	CentreWest - Westbourne Park	Cummins engine fitted in 1990, refurbished in 1994
2507	London Central - New Cross	Cummins engine fitted in 1990, refurbished in 1993
2508	Metroline - Willesden	Cummins engine fitted in 1993, refurbished in 1993
2509	Metroline - Willesden	Cummins engine fitted in 1992, refurbished in 1992
2510	Leaside Buses - Tottenham	Cummins engine fitted in 1991, refurbished in 1993
2511	MTL London - Holloway	Cummins engine fitted in 1991, refurbished in 1993
2512	Kentish Bus- Battersea	Iveco engine fitted in 1992, refurbished in 1993
2513	London Central - Camberwell	Cummins engine fitted in 1991, refurbished in 1994
2514	Kentish Bus- Battersea	Iveco engine fitted in 1992, refurbished in 1993
2515	London Central - Camberwell	Cummins engine fitted in 1991, refurbished in 1993
2516	London General - Waterloo	Iveco engine fitted in 1991, refurbished in 1993, doors fitted & reclassified DRM in 1991, re-reg WLT516 in 1994
2517	London General - Waterloo	Iveco engine fitted in 1991, refurbished in 1992
2518	Leaside Buses - Tottenham	Cummins engine fitted in 1990, refurbished in 1993
2519	London United - Shepherds Bush	Cummins engine fitted in 1993, refurbished in 1993
2520	London General - Putney	Iveco engine fitted in 1991, refurbished in 1992
2521	South London - Brixton	Iveco engine fitted in 1991, refurbished in 1993
2522	CentreWest - Westbourne Park	Cummins engine fitted in 1990, refurbished in 1993
2523	Kentish Bus- Battersea	Iveco engine fitted in 1992, refurbished in 1993
2524	Kentish Bus- Battersea	Iveco engine fitted in 1990, refurbished in 1993
2525	Leaside Buses - Tottenham	Cummins engine fitted in 1991, refurbished in 1994
2526	Leaside Buses - Clapton	Cummins engine fitted in 1991, refurbished in 1992
2527	BTS Coaches - Borehamwood	Cummins engine fitted in 1991, refurbished in 1993
2528	Leaside Buses - Tottenham	Cummins engine fitted in 1991, refurbished in 1993
2529	London Central - Camberwell	Cummins engine fitted in 1990, refurbished in 1992
2530	CentreWest - Westbourne Park	Cummins engine fitted in 1990, refurbished in 1993
2531	Kentish Bus- Battersea	Iveco engine fitted in 1990, refurbished in 1993
2532	Metroline - Willesden	Cummins engine fitted in 1991, refurbished in 1993
2533	Kentish Bus- Battersea	Iveco engine fitted in 1991, refurbished in 1993
2534	Leaside Buses - Clapton	Cummins engine fitted in 1991, refurbished in 1992
2535	London General - Putney	Iveco engine fitted in 1991, refurbished in 1992
2536	Kentish Bus- Battersea	Iveco engine fitted in 1992, refurbished in 1993
2537	Metroline - Willesden	Cummins engine fitted in 1992,refurbished in 1993
2538	BTS Coaches - Borehamwood	Cummins engine fitted in 1992, refurbished in 1993
2539	London Central - New Cross	Cummins engine fitted in 1992, refurbished in 1993
2540	London General - Putney	Iveco engine fitted in 1991, refurbished in 1993
2541	Stagecoach East London - Upton Park	Cummins engine fitted in 1990, refurbished in 1992
2542	CentreWest - Westbourne Park	Cummins engine fitted in 1990, refurbished in 1992
2543	London General - Putney	Iveco engine fitted in 1991, refurbished in 1993
2544	Leaside Buses - Tottenham	Cummins engine fitted in 1991, refurbished and new offside illuminated advert panels fitted in 1992
2545	South London - Brixton	Iveco engine fitted in 1992, refurbished in 1993
2546	Leaside Buses - Tottenham	Cummins engine fitted in 1991, refurbished in 1993
2547	Metroline - Willesden	Cummins engine fitted in 1993, refurbished in 1993
2548	Kentish Bus- Battersea	Iveco engine fitted in 1991, refurbished in 1993
2549	South London - Brixton	Iveco engine fitted in 1991, refurbished in 1992
2550	Stagecoach East London - Upton Park	Cummins engine fitted in 1990, refurbished in 1993
2551	London Central - Camberwell	Cummins engine fitted in 1991, refurbished in 1992
2552	Leaside Buses - Clapton	Cummins engine fitted in 1990, refurbished in 1992
2553	CentreWest - Westbourne Park	Cummins engine fitted in 1990, refurbished in 1993
2554	London Central - Camberwell	Cummins engine fitted in 1990, refurbished in 1992
2555	CentreWest - Westbourne Park	Cummins engine fitted in 1991, refurbished in 1992
2556	London Central - Camberwell	Cummins engine fitted in 1990, refurbished in 1994
2558	Metroline - Willesden	Cummins engine fitted in 1992, refurbished in 1993
2559	CentreWest - Westbourne Park	Cummins engine fitted in 1990, refurbished in 1994
2560	London Central - Camberwell	Cummins engine fitted in 1991, refurbished in 1992
2561	MTL London - Holloway	Cummins engine fitted in 1991, refurbished in 1992
2562	Leaside Buses - Tottenham	Cummins engine fitted in 1990, refurbished in 1994
2563	BTS Coaches - Borehamwood	Cummins engine fitted in 1991, refurbished in 1993

2564	London General - Putney	Iveco engine fitted in 1991, refurbished in 1992
2565	Stagecoach East London - Upton Park	Cummins engine fitted in 1991, refurbished in 1992
2566	Metroline - Willesden	Cummins engine fitted in 1990, refurbished in 1993
2567	Leaside Buses - Clapton	Cummins engine fitted in 1990, refurbished in 1992
2568	London General - Putney	Iveco engine fitted in 1991, refurbished in 1993
2569	BTS Coaches - Borehamwood	Cummins engine fitted in 1991, refurbished in 1993
2570	London General - Putney	Iveco engine fitted in 1991, refurbished in 1993
2571	Leaside Buses - Tottenham	Cummins engine fitted in 1991, refurbished in 1993
2572	South London - Brixton	Iveco engine fitted in 1991, refurbished in 1993
2573	South London - Brixton	Iveco engine fitted in 1991, refurbished in 1994
2574	Kentish Bus- Battersea	Iveco engine fitted in 1990, refurbished in 1993
2575	London General - Putney	Iveco engine fitted in 1990, refurbished in 1992
2576	London General - Putney	Iveco engine fitted in 1991, refurbished in 1992
2577	Kentish Bus- Battersea	Iveco engine fitted in 1990, refurbished in 1993
2578	London Central - New Cross	Cummins engine fitted in 1990, refurbished in 1993
2579	Metroline - Willesden	Cummins engine fitted in 1993, refurbished in 1993
2580	London General - Putney	Iveco engine fitted in 1990, refurbished in 1993
2581	Stagecoach East London - Upton Park	Cummins engine fitted in 1991, refurbished in 1993
2582	BTS Coaches - Borehamwood	Cummins engine fitted in 1991, refurbished in 1993
2583	London Central - New Cross	Cummins engine fitted in 1990, refurbished in 1992
2584	London Central - New Cross	Cummins engine fitted in 1991, refurbished in 1994
2585	Metroline - Willesden	Cummins engine fitted in 1993, refurbished in 1994
2586	Kentish Bus- Battersea	Iveco engine fitted in 1990, refurbished in 1993
2587	London Central - Camberwell	Cummins engine fitted in 1991, refurbished in 1992
2588	Leaside Buses - Tottenham	Cummins engine fitted in 1991, refurbished and new offside illuminated advert panels fitted in 1992
2589	Leaside Buses - Tottenham	Cummins engine fitted in 1991, refurbished in 1994
2590	London General - Putney	Iveco engine fitted in 1991, refurbished in 1993
2591	Kentish Bus- Battersea	Iveco engine fitted in 1990, refurbished in 1993
2592	Stagecoach East London - Bow	Iveco engine fitted in 1992, refurbished in 1992
2593	London General - Putney	Iveco engine fitted in 1991, refurbished in 1993
2594	Metroline - Willesden	Cummins engine fitted in 1992, refurbished in 1993
2595	Leaside Buses - Tottenham	Cummins engine fitted in 1990, refurbished in 1992
2596	London Central - New Cross	Cummins engine fitted in 1991, refurbished in 1994
2597	Leaside Buses - Clapton	Cummins engine fitted in 1991, refurbished in 1992
2598	BTS Coaches - Borehamwood	Cummins engine fitted in 1990, refurbished in 1993
2599	Metroline - Willesden	Cummins engine fitted in 1993, refurbished in 1994
2600	London United - Shepherds Bush	Cummins engine fitted in 1992, refurbished in 1993
2601	London Central - Camberwell	Cummins engine fitted in 1991, refurbished in 1993
2602	CentreWest - Westbourne Park	Cummins engine fitted in 1992, refurbished in 1994
2603	MTL London - Holloway	Cummins engine fitted in 1991, refurbished in 1992
2604	London Central - New Cross	Cummins engine fitted in 1990, refurbished in 1993
2605	London General - Putney	Iveco engine fitted in 1991, refurbished in 1992
2606	London General - Waterloo	Iveco engine fitted in 1991, refurbished in 1993
2607	Stagecoach East London - Bow	Iveco engine fitted in 1992, refurbished in 1993
2608	South London - Brixton	Iveco engine fitted in 1991, refurbished in 1992
2609	CentreWest - Westbourne Park	Cummins engine fitted in 1990, refurbished in 1993
2610	Stagecoach East London - Upton Park	Cummins engine fitted in 1991, refurbished in 1993
2611	Leaside Buses - Tottenham	Cummins engine fitted in 1990, refurbished in 1992
2612	London General - Putney	Iveco engine fitted in 1990, refurbished in 1993
2613	London Central - New Cross	Cummins engine fitted in 1991, refurbished in 1992
2614	London Central - Camberwell	Cummins engine fitted in 1991, refurbished in 1993
2615	London General - Putney	Iveco engine fitted in 1990, refurbished in 1992
2616	Stagecoach East London - Upton Park	Cummins engine fitted in 1991, refurbished in 1992
2617	Leaside Buses - Tottenham	Cummins engine fitted in 1991, refurbished in 1994
2618	London General - Waterloo	Turbocharged Iveco engine fitted in 1992, refurbished in 1993
2619	Kentish Bus- Battersea	Iveco engine fitted in 1991, refurbished in 1993
2620	MTL London - Holloway	Cummins engine fitted in 1991, refurbished in 1993
2621	London United - Shepherds Bush	Cummins engine fitted in 1992, refurbished in 1992
2622	London United - Shepherds Bush	Cummins engine fitted in 1993, refurbished in 1993
2623	CentreWest - Westbourne Park	Cummins engine fitted in 1991, refurbished in 1994
2624	Stagecoach East London - Bow	Iveco engine fitted in 1992, refurbished in 1992

2625	Leaside Buses - Tottenham	Cummins engine fitted in 1991, refurbished in 1993
2626	London General - Putney	Iveco engine fitted in 1991, refurbished in 1992
2627	BTS Coaches - Borehamwood	Cummins engine fitted in 1992, refurbished in 1993
2628	Leaside Buses - Tottenham	Cummins engine fitted in 1990, refurbished in 1994
2629	London Central - Camberwell	Cummins engine fitted in 1993, refurbished in 1993
2630	London Central - Camberwell	Cummins engine fitted in 1990, refurbished in 1994
2631	London General - Putney	Iveco engine fitted in 1991, refurbished in 1993
2632	Leaside Buses - Tottenham	Cummins engine fitted in 1991, refurbished in 1993
2633	BTS Coaches - Borehamwood	Cummins engine fitted in 1993, refurbished in 1993
2634	Metroline - Willesden	Cummins engine fitted in 1993, refurbished in 1994
2635	Leaside Buses - Tottenham	Cummins engine fitted in 1991, refurbished in 1993
2636	South London - Brixton	Iveco engine fitted in 1991, refurbished in 1994
2637	London General - Putney	Iveco engine fitted in 1991, refurbished in 1993
2638	Leaside Buses - Tottenham	Cummins engine fitted in 1991, refurbished in 1993
2639	Stagecoach East London - Upton Park	Cummins engine fitted in 1991, refurbished in 1992
2640	London General - Putney	Iveco engine fitted in 1991, refurbished in 1992
2641	Stagecoach East London - Upton Park	Cummins engine fitted in 1991, refurbished in 1992
2642	Stagecoach East London - Upton Park	Cummins engine fitted in 1990, refurbished in 1993
2643	Leaside Buses - Tottenham	Cummins engine fitted in 1991, refurbished in 1992
2644	London General - Putney	Iveco engine fitted in 1991, refurbished in 1992
2645	London United - Shepherds Bush	Cummins engine fitted in 1990, refurbished in 1992
2646	London United - Shepherds Bush	Cummins engine fitted in 1992, refurbished in 1993
2647	CentreWest - Westbourne Park	Cummins engine fitted in 1990, refurbished in 1992
2648	London General - Waterloo	Iveco engine fitted in 1991, refurbished in 1994
2649	Metroline - Willesden	Cummins engine fitted in 1991, refurbished in 1993
2650	London United - Shepherds Bush	Cummins engine fitted in 1991, refurbished in 1992
2651	Metroline - Willesden	Cummins engine fitted in 1993, refurbished in 1993
2652	Metroline - Willesden	Cummins engine fitted in 1992, refurbished in 1993
2653	South London - Brixton	Iveco engine fitted in 1991, refurbished in 1994
2654	London General - Putney	Iveco engine fitted in 1990, refurbished in 1992
2655	Leaside Buses - Tottenham	Cummins engine fitted in 1990, refurbished in 1993
2656	CentreWest - Westbourne Park	Cummins engine fitted in 1991, refurbished in 1994
2657	Stagecoach East London - Bow	Iveco engine fitted in 1992, refurbished in 1992
2658	Leaside Buses - Tottenham	Cummins engine fitted in 1990, refurbished in 1992
2659	BTS Coaches - Borehamwood	Cummins engine fitted in 1993, refurbished in 1993
2660	Leaside Buses - Tottenham	Cummins engine fitted in 1991, refurbished in 1993
2661	Stagecoach East London - Upton Park	Cummins engine fitted in 1991, refurbished in 1992
2662	London United - Shepherds Bush	Cummins engine fitted in 1991, refurbished in 1992
2663	BTS Coaches - Borehamwood	Cummins engine fitted in 1993, refurbished in 1993
2664	CentreWest - Westbourne Park	Cummins engine fitted in 1990, refurbished in 1994
2665	Stagecoach East London - Bow	Iveco engine fitted in 1992, refurbished in 1993
2666	Leaside Buses - Tottenham	Cummins engine fitted in 1990, refurbished in 1994
2667	CentreWest - Westbourne Park	Cummins engine fitted in 1993, refurbished in 1994
2668	BTS Coaches - Borehamwood	Cummins engine fitted in 1992, refurbished in 1993
2669	London General - Waterloo	Iveco engine fitted in 1990, refurbished in 1992
2670	Stagecoach East London - Upton Park	Cummins engine fitted in 1991, refurbished in 1993
2671	Stagecoach East London - Upton Park	Cummins engine fitted in 1991, refurbished in 1992
2672	CentreWest - Westbourne Park	Cummins engine fitted in 1990, refurbished in 1994
2673	London Central - New Cross	Cummins engine fitted in 1991, refurbished in 1993
2674	BTS Coaches - Borehamwood	Cummins engine fitted in 1992, refurbished in 1993
2675	Leaside Buses - Clapton	Cummins engine fitted in 1991, refurbished in 1992
2676	London Central - Camberwell	Cummins engine fitted in 1993, refurbished in 1993
2677	CentreWest - Westbourne Park	Cummins engine fitted in 1992, refurbished in 1992
2678	Leaside Buses - Tottenham	Cummins engine fitted in 1991, refurbished in 1993
2679	MTL London - Holloway	Cummins engine fitted in 1990, refurbished in 1992
2680	London General - Waterloo	Iveco engine fitted in 1991, refurbished in 1993
2681	Metroline - Willesden	Cummins engine fitted in 1993, refurbished in 1993
2682	Leaside Buses - Clapton	Cummins engine fitted in 1992, refurbished in 1993
2683	London Central - Camberwell	Cummins engine fitted in 1991, refurbished in 1992
2684	Leaside Buses - Tottenham	Cummins engine fitted in 1991, refurbished in 1994
2685	Leaside Buses - Clapton	Cummins engine fitted in 1990, refurbished in 1992
2686	BTS Coaches - Borehamwood	Cummins engine fitted in 1991, refurbished in 1993
2687	CentreWest - Westbourne Park	Cummins engine fitted in 1991, refurbished in 1993
2688	Leaside Buses - Clapton	Cummins engine fitted in 1992, refurbished in 1993

2689	Metroline - Willesden	Cummins engine fitted in 1992, refurbished in 1992
2690	Metroline - Willesden	Cummins engine fitted in 1990, refurbished in 1994
2691	Gala Cosmetics, Finland	location and recent use unknown, registered PI-187
2692	South London - Brixton	Iveco engine fitted in 1991, refurbished in 1993
2693	London General - Waterloo	Iveco engine fitted in 1990, refurbished in 1992
2694	BTS Coaches - Borehamwood	Cummins engine fitted in 1993, refurbished in 1993
2695	Metroline - Willesden	Cummins engine fitted in 1991, refurbished in 1994
2696	Stagecoach East London - Bow	Iveco engine fitted and refurbished in 1994
2697	London United - Shepherds Bush	Cummins engine fitted in 1990, refurbished in 1992
2698	Metroline - Willesden	Cummins engine fitted in 1994, refurbished in 1994
2699	MTL London - Holloway	Cummins engine fitted in 1991, refurbished in 1992
2700	London United - Shepherds Bush	Cummins engine fitted in 1993, refurbished in 1993
2701	Metroline - Willesden	Cummins engine fitted in 1992, refurbished in 1992
2702	London United - Shepherds Bush	Cummins engine fitted in 1992, refurbished in 1993
2703	Metroline - Willesden	Cummins engine fitted in 1992, refurbished in 1993
2704	London United - Shepherds Bush	Cummins engine fitted in 1990, refurbished in 1992
2705	Stagecoach East London - Upton Park	Cummins engine fitted in 1991, refurbished in 1992
2706	Metroline - Willesden	Cummins engine fitted in 1992, refurbished in 1993
2707	London United - Shepherds Bush	Cummins engine fitted in 1991, refurbished in 1992
2708	Leaside Buses - Tottenham	Cummins engine fitted in 1990, refurbished in 1993
2709	Stagecoach East London - Bow	Iveco engine fitted in 1992, refurbished in 1993
2710	Metroline - Willesden	Cummins engine fitted in 1993, refurbished in 1993
2711	London Central - Camberwell	Cummins engine fitted in 1991, refurbished in 1992
2712	London Central - Camberwell	Cummins engine fitted in 1991, refurbished in 1992
2713	Metroline - Willesden	Cummins engine fitted in 1993, refurbished in 1993
2714	London Central - Camberwell	Cummins engine fitted in 1991, refurbished in 1994
2715	Kentish Bus- Battersea	Iveco engine fitted in 1990, refurbished in 1993
2716	Leaside Buses - Clapton	Cummins engine fitted in 1990, refurbished in 1993
2717	CentreWest - Westbourne Park	Cummins engine fitted in 1991, refurbished in 1993
2718	South London - Brixton	Iveco engine fitted in 1991, refurbished in 1992
2719	BTS Coaches - Borehamwood	Cummins engine fitted in 1991, refurbished in 1993
2720	London United - Shepherds Bush	Cummins engine fitted in 1991, refurbished in 1992
2721	London United - Shepherds Bush	Cummins engine fitted in 1993, refurbished in 1993
2722	London United - Shepherds Bush	Cummins engine fitted in 1991, refurbished in 1992
2723	Stagecoach East London - Upton Park	Cummins engine fitted in 1991, refurbished in 1992
2724	CentreWest - Westbourne Park	Cummins engine fitted in 1990, refurbished in 1993
2725	London General - Waterloo	Iveco engine fitted in 1991, refurbished in 1992
2726	South London - Brixton	Iveco engine fitted in 1990, refurbished in 1994
2727	Metroline - Willesden	Cummins engine fitted in 1990, refurbished in 1993
2728	Metroline - Willesden	Cummins engine fitted in 1992, refurbished in 1993
2729	London United - Shepherds Bush	Cummins engine fitted in 1991, refurbished in 1992
2730	South London - Brixton	Iveco engine fitted in 1990, refurbished in 1992
2731	MTL London - Holloway	Cummins engine fitted in 1991, refurbished in 1992
2732	London General - Waterloo	Iveco engine fitted in 1991, refurbished in 1993
2733	London Central - Camberwell	Cummins engine fitted in 1991, refurbished in 1992
2734	London United - Shepherds Bush	Cummins engine fitted in 1991, refurbished in 1992
2735	CentreWest - Westbourne Park	Cummins engine fitted in 1991, refurbished in 1994
2736	London General - Waterloo	Iveco engine fitted in 1991, refurbished in 1993
2737	Metroline - Willesden	Cummins engine fitted in 1991, refurbished in 1994
2738	Stagecoach East London - Bow	Iveco engine fitted in 1992, refurbished in 1993
2739	London United - Shepherds Bush	Cummins engine fitted in 1993, refurbished in 1993
2740	CentreWest - Westbourne Park	Cummins engine fitted in 1991, refurbished in 1993
2741	South London - Brixton	Iveco engine fitted in 1991, refurbished in 1992
2742	Leaside Buses - Tottenham	Cummins engine fitted in 1991, refurbished in 1993
2743	Stagecoach East London - Upton Park	Cummins engine fitted in 1991, refurbished in 1993
2744	London United - Shepherds Bush	Cummins engine fitted in 1992, refurbished in 1992
2745	London General - Putney	Iveco engine fitted in 1991, air brakes fitted in 1992, refurbished in 1993
2746	Leaside Buses - Tottenham	Cummins engine fitted in 1990, refurbished in 1993
2747	Leaside Buses - Tottenham	Cummins engine fitted in 1990, refurbished in 1993
2748	Stagecoach East London - Upton Park	Cummins engine fitted in 1990, refurbished in 1993
2749	Stagecoach East London - Bow	Iveco engine fitted in 1992, refurbished in 1993
2750	Leaside Buses - Clapton	Cummins engine fitted in 1993, refurbished in 1993
2751	London United - Shepherds Bush	Cummins engine fitted in 1990, refurbished in 1992

2752	London General - Waterloo	Iveco engine fitted in 1991, refurbished in 1992
2753	South London - Brixton	Iveco engine fitted in 1991, refurbished in 1993
2754	Leaside Buses - Clapton	Cummins engine fitted in 1993, refurbished in 1993
2755	Metroline - Willesden	Cummins engine fitted in 1991, refurbished in 1994
2756	BTS Coaches - Borehamwood	Cummins engine fitted in 1992, refurbished in 1994
2757	London United - Shepherds Bush	Cummins engine fitted in 1993, refurbished in 1993
2758	Leaside Buses - Clapton	Cummins engine fitted and refurbished in 1994
2759	South London - Brixton	Iveco engine fitted in 1991, refurbished in 1993
2760	Stagecoach East London - Upton Park	Traditional style refurbishment in 1990

At the time of writing, some RMs remained whole or in semi-whole condition in the scrap yard of PVS at Barnsley after the sale of some 50 RMs for scrap from London Buses at the end of 1994. The vehicles in question are not included in the listing. Included in this collection of vehicles is former showbus RM14. PVS at Barnsley became the final resting place for the majority of all scrap Routemasters following the signing of a contract with London Buses in 1984.

Facts and Figures

Type	Length	Width	Height	Wheelbase	Weight	Seating Capacity	
RM	27' 6^1/$_2$"	7' 11^1/$_2$"	14' 4^1/$_2$"	16' 10"	7366 kg	H36/28R	
RM	27' 6^1/$_2$"	7' 11^1/$_2$"	13' 9"	16' 10"	7021 kg	O36/28R	(open top)
RMC	27' 6^1/$_2$"	7' 11^1/$_2$"	14' 4^1/$_2$"	16' 10"	7874 kg	H32/25RD	
RMC	27' 6^1/$_2$"	7' 11^1/$_2$"	13' 9"	16' 10"	varies	O32/25RD	(open top)
RCL	29' 10^1/$_2$"	7' 11^1/$_2$"	14' 5"	19' 2"	8255 kg	varies	
RCL	29' 10^1/$_2$"	7' 11^1/$_2$"	14' 5"	19' 2"	8255 kg	varies	(convertible)
RML	29' 10^1/$_2$"	7' 11^1/$_2$"	14' 5"	19' 2"	7874 kg	H40/32R	
DRM	29' 10^1/$_2$"	7' 11^1/$_2$"	14' 5"	19' 2"	7951 kg	H40/32RD	
RMA	27' 6^1/$_2$"	7' 11^1/$_2$"	14' 4^1/$_2$"	16' 10"	7823 kg	H32/24F	
ERM	31' 8"	7' 11^1/$_2$"	13' 9"	21' 6"	7660 kg	O44/32R	(open top)
RMF	29' 10^1/$_2$"	7' 11^1/$_2$"	14' 4^1/$_2$"	19' 2"	8200 kg	H41/31F	
RMF	29' 10^1/$_2$"	7' 11^1/$_2$"	13' 9"	19' 2"	7600 kg	O41/31F	(open top)
FRM	31' 3"	7' 11^1/$_2$"	14' 5"	16' 10"	8636 kg	H41/31F	

RMC4 length is 27' 3^1/$_2$" and weight is 7620kg and RMF1254 is H38/31F.

REGISTRATION INDEX (for vehicles in the United Kingdom only)

XFF 258, 813, 814	RM10, RML898, 890.
XVS 319, 826, 828, 830, 839, 850, 851	RM949, 648, 843, 180, 244, 1083, 467.
XYJ 418, 419, 427-430, 440	RM736, 625, 1185, 32, 1205, 1070, 838.
YVS 285 - 294	RM1134, 809, 1053, 357, 55, 1149, 219, 1032, 447, 229.
71 AWN	RM1397.
100BXL	RM1000.
1, 3, 9, 33, 58, 62, 63, 69, 81, 82, 87, 97, 102, 104, 109, 119, 123, 138, 152, 158, 159, 168, 171, 174, 176, 183, 204, 209, 214, 218, 260, 280, 283, 287, 305, 314, 321, 324, 348, 353, 357, 363, 368, 380, 394, 400, 403, 414, 428, 449, 527, 543, 562, 563, 568, 571, 583, 590, 593 CLT	RM1001 etc.
254 CLT	RMF1254.
453, 459, 461, 462, 464, 469, 474, 476, 477, 485, 487, 490, 492, 495, 496, 497, 507, 510, 513, 515, 516 CLT	RMC1453 etc.
627, 640, 641, 643, 650, 653, 654, 666, 676, 677, 691, 699, 725, 727, 731, 734, 735, 737, 747, 758, 767, 771, 776, 783, 790, 797, 799, 801, 822, 825, 840, 859, 864 DYE	RM1627 etc.
ABD 892A	RM1068.
AEW 440A	RM1421.
ALC 290, 368, 464A	RM1005, RMC1500, RML902.
AST 415, 416A	RM45, 191.
BNK 32A	RM1647.
DFH 806A	RM969.
EDS 50, 98, 221, 288, 300, 320A	RM560, 1006, 1010, 910, 388, 606.
KGH 858, 925, 975A	RM1125, 1078, 1330.
KGJ 117, 118, 142, 167, 187A	RM1528, 1398, 311, 1700, 1621.
LDS 67, 164, 201, 210, 236, 237, 238, 239, 261, 279, 280, 282, 284, 337, 341, 402A	RM1274, 978, 1607, 1245, 272, 416, 697, 727, 956, 54, 104, 245, 546, 364, 441, 1145
NKH 807A	RM1366.
NRH 801, 802, 803, 805A	RM732, 798, 871, 1041.
NSG 636A	RM1164.
OYM 368, 453A	RM1002, 29.
PAG 809A	RM1741.
WTS 102, 186, 225, 245, 404, 418A	RM917, 1143, 943, 298, 702, 909.
XMD 81A	RM429.
XSL 220, 596A	RM26, 1289.
YTS 820, 824, 973A	RM1599, 321, 1017.
ALD 871, 872, 878, 913, 919, 933, 936, 941, 948, 955, 962, 966, 968, 971, 975, 977, 978, 979, 980, 983, 989, 990, 993B	RM1871 etc.
ALM 11, 21, 22, 23, 24, 33, 34, 37, 41, 50, 51, 59, 60, 65, 71, 78, 83, 89, 90, 97, 103B	RM2011 etc.
BFW 544B	RM1842.
EDS 537, 620B	RM1630, 2081.

EGF 220, 285B	RM1811, 1836.
EVM 132B	RM1807.
EUP 405B	ex NGT 2105.
EYY 327B	RM1804.
CUV 106, 107, 109, 116, 121, 122, 124, 128, 136, 151, 153, 154, 156, 173, 178, 179, 180, 185, 186, 192, 198, 201, 203, 208, 210, 213, 217C	RM2106 etc.
CUV 218 - 221, 223, 226, 229, 233, 235, 238 - 241, 243, 245, 248, 250, 253, 254, 256, 259, 260C	RCL2218 etc.
CUV 261-305C	RML2261-2305.
CUV 307-318C	RML2307-2318.
CUV 321-336C	RML2321-2336.
CUV 338-363C	RML2338-2363.
FPT 581, 588, 590, 592, 603C	ex NGT2111, 2118, 2120, 2122, 2133.
KGJ 601 - 603, 611, 612, 614, 621, 622D	RMA28, 14, 29, 15, 37, 16, 1, 19.
JJD 364-416D	RML2364-2416.
JJD 418, 419, 422D	RML2418, 2419, 2422.
JJD 428-432D	RML2428-2432.
JJD 434, 435, 437D	RML2434, 2435, 2437.
JJD 439-447D	RML2439-2447.
JJD 450-457D	RML2450-2457.
JJD 460-556D	RML2460-2556.
JJD 558-598D	RML2558-2598.
KGY 4D	FRM1.
NML 599-657E	RML2599-2657.
NMY 630, 631, 632, 634, 635, 636, 637, 638, 640, 641, 644, 646, 647, 648, 649, 654, 655, 656, 662, 665E	RMA47, 48, 49, 50, 5, 51, 52, 6, 8, 53, 55, 9, 10, 11, 23, 57, 58, 13, 62, 65
SMK 658-690F	RML2658-2690.
SMK 692-760F	RML2692-2760